W9-AHF-203

Just Pencil Me In

Your Guide to Moving & Getting Settled After 60

Quill
Driver
Books

Sanger, California

Printed in the United States of America

Published by Quill Driver Books/Word Dancer Press, Inc.

1831 Industrial Way, #101

Sanger, California 93657

559-876-2170 • 1-800-497-4909 • FAX 559-876-2180

QuillDriverBooks.com

Quill Driver Books titles may be purchased in quantity at special discounts for educational, fund-raising, business, or promotional use. Please contact Special Markets, Quill Driver Books/Word Dancer Press, Inc. at the above address, toll-free at 1-800-497-4909 or by e-mail: Info@QuillDriverBooks.com

Quill Driver Books/Word Dancer Press, Inc. project cadre:
Doris Hall, John David Marion, Stephen Blake Mettee, Linda Kay Weber.

First Printing 2002

To order another copy of this book, please call
1-800-497-4909

Library of Congress Cataloging-in-Publication Data

Gore, Willma Willis.
    Just pencil me in : a guide to moving and settling in after 60 / by Willma Willis Gore.
        p. cm.
    Includes bibliographical references and index.
    ISBN 1-884956-21-1
    1. Moving, Household. 2. Aged—Housing. I. Title.

TX307 .G67 2002
648'.9—dc21   2002005202

To friend and mentor, Audrey Yanes,
who shares my memories and hopes
and does her best to keep me moving right along
and
to my children, Greg, Jim, John, Alan, Andy, David, Janice and Jill who
have taken all Mom's moves in stride

Contents

4

A Moveable Feast of Choices

5

Memorable Moves

6

7

8

9

The Stuff Sale 105

10

Shape Up and Move Out 117

Introduction

Last spring I moved body, bed, desk, files, clothing—all my material possessions—again! To make light of the messes I regularly cause in friends' and relatives' address books, I sent the news in rhyme:

> Use caution! As it's always been,
> Save your ink. Just pencil me in.

This latest move was the twentieth move in my peripatetic life and the sixth since my seventieth birthday. Shortly before that birthday, and a few months after the death of my husband, I sold our suburban home and pared down a large household of furnishings to what would fit in a U-Haul van.

I had visited a resort in the San Bernardino Mountains of California many times—the site of hiking adventures when the children were young. To launch my new beginning, I purchased a small home there on a tree-sheltered slope.

Friends closest to me cautioned: "You won't know anybody!" Implying, of course, that I was "too old" to start over. Ha!

In a lifetime of living in a dozen cities and hamlets from Los Angeles to Gadsden, Alabama, I've found exciting people everywhere. Reach out with friendship and it is returned. I still correspond with people I've befriended in various places over a fifty-year span.

Six moves since seventy? Well, practice in packing makes it easier, of course, but I've learned many practical and innovative moving techniques and shortcuts along the way. And, with this book, I'm betting that what I've learned will be of value to others of six-plus decades who are considering launching themselves off on moves to new vistas and new adventures that will likely make this time the best years of their lives.

1
Why Move?

We often liken any nearly impossible task to moving a mountain. Since few of us are skilled in the use of dynamite or backhoes, we feel safely exempt from ever having, literally, to do this. Moving a household, however—whether cabin or mansion—strikes most people as equivalent to uprooting Mount Rushmore. And yet, it should come as no surprise that our society is far more mobile now than ever in the past. More than eight million households change addresses every year and 4.5 million of the over-fifty population in the United States move in an average year.

Now that We're Superadults

As we reach our fiftiess and sixties, some superadults (new terminology for those who object to being called "seniors") tend to think it's time to settle in for the duration of our lives. For others—and not only the snowbird crowd—moving from place to place may be both necessary and the source of wonderful new adventures. My advice is to welcome the opportunity. Each move may be the best thing you ever do for yourself—or yourselves—if "you" are a couple.

All moves require a kind of independence that may have become rusty from lack of practice—but there is a payoff in personal satisfaction and pride of accomplishment. Among the most valuable aspects of independence is that it brings a great sense of liberation.

For me, the simple advantages of moving are these: I do what I want, when I want. I've happily survived the challenges and consequences of twenty moves in forty years. Every move has brought me new friends, new ideas, new activities I hadn't before imagined.

For those who have lived in one home in one community for the major part of their lives, the very thought of leaving it may be intimidating, but it's also the opportunity to clear out the accumulated refuse of many years and pare down to more manageable bulk. The proliferation of garage sales demonstrates that the human animal chronically accumulates more than he needs.

But don't sell off everything. Objects to save are family photos and records and period pieces of monetary and/or sentimental value. However, even some of these may be stored for future retrieval. (See Chapter 8, "Dealing With Stuff Overload.")

What I have learned in my many moves is supplemented here by examples of moves—both ideal and misguided—reported by those I've met along the van-line-crowded highways. Sharing these experiences is the purpose of this book.

No matter what the reason for a move or how undesirable the destination appears at first, changes in the better half of our lives may require relocating and relocating. When, why, where and how? As we will see, options abound.

Reasons We Move

Loss of a partner or changes in your health may be your primary motive for moving. Other reasons may range from staying ahead of the law (though in that case you probably wouldn't have time for this book) to the desire to be nearer (or farther from!) your kids, a desire for change of scenery, financial considerations, or merely a restless yen to hit the road.

Loss of Spouse/Partner

When two people share the responsibilities of a home—whether it's a small house or multiple acres of retirement dream—the joy of sharing makes the tasks worthwhile. Yet when one is left to manage alone, regardless of sentimental attachments, it may be time for a change.

My husband and I were in our sixties when, though reluctant to do so, we left our four-bedroom Victorian country home. His health had deteriorated and he could no longer share the upkeep of our five acres. We sold the property and moved to a smaller house in town. It was big enough to welcome visits from kids—if all didn't come at once—and it had a yard the right size for puttering but not so large as to be a burden to either of us. This move proved both wise and prophetic. He died two years later.

Learning to live alone—at any age—is bewildering at first. Some, devastated by loss of the spouse, can, nonetheless, take over and manage responsibilities formerly left to the partner. Others, besides mourning the loss of a companion, simply don't know how to manage anything more complicated than getting to the barber or the hairdresser. If that's your category—don't despair. You are among friends—more than you can imagine. Help is as near as these chapters, your telephone, or the World Wide Web.

Though we had lived in our community for twenty years, I wanted to reduce responsibilities for household management after my husband's death. I was seventy at the time and in good health. While I had many dear friends in the area, the nice little country town had grown into a city with accompanying smog and traffic. I yearned for a higher elevation and a change of scene. I sold that home and purchased a—perfect for me—mountain retreat, 250 miles away. I did not lose old friends by moving away from them. Four moves later, I still keep in contact and visit them often.

Health Considerations

As fit as any of us may feel at fifty, sixty, seventy, or eighty, glowing health is not likely to remain in full force through our *entire* first century—Jack La Lanne notwithstanding. The common late-life condition of high blood pressure may require that we move from a high elevation to one nearer sea level. Late-life allergies, broken bones, or chronic illnesses may beset us. A move may be needed to alleviate symptoms or gain better accessibility to special care or to the kind of attention that monitors us but does not invade our privacy.

The annual change of seasons was a major reason my friends Marge and Steve loved their Northern California home. However, at sixty-five and sixty-seven they took the advice of their family doctor who detected a heart murmur in Steve and recommended a future knee replacement for Marge. These conditions suggested that raking leaves and shoveling snow-blanketed driveways were no longer advisable. The couple decided to move to a climate where such efforts were unnecessary.

To Join the Kids—Or Not?

Our loved ones are, in the best situations, the greatest sources of comfort when we are ill or needful for any reason. If—through our own choices or theirs—we become separated by miles, states, or continents, the need or the desire to be nearer may be overwhelming and warp our good judgment.

Young adults seeking their fortunes tend to move around a lot. Consider, if after moving once to be near your child, if your child and his or her family were to relocate yet again, would you be willing to pull up roots yourself and move? Or would you be willing to remain in a new, relatively unfamiliar locale? It is not always the best plan to follow your children to a new community.

An example of following the kids comes from my friend Marian. She retired at sixty-five from an accounting position in Portland, Oregon, and moved to be near her daughter on the Central Coast of California.

Within three months after Marian settled a few blocks from her daughter, the young woman got a promotion that took her to another state. Fortunately, before Marian followed, she and the widower husband of an old friend found each other. Both gregarious, they organized a social group for widows and widowers. Marian tells me that in the past two years they've celebrated the weddings of three couples who met at the senior center. She and her widower are soon to be the fourth couple to commit to each other. They are in

Plan with Your Finances in Mind

If you plan for moving costs properly, at least half the burdens of a move are lifted. Careful planners will weigh the costs not only of the transfer but the arrival. Even a do-it-yourself move will add $500 to $5,000 or more to your expenditures compared to the normal costs of remaining where you are. The initial setup at a new location—outlay for a new telephone number, TV, electricity, and gas connections may total more than the monthly utility bills you have been paying. A bit of useful wisdom I've gleaned in my moving career has been that, no matter how carefully planned, any major change winds up costing more than anticipated.

My fixed income did not change with a move I made to California's Central Coast, but overall there

their early seventies. Yes, Marian will move again—this time into his home. Following her daughter the first time turned out happily for Marian. The main reason was that she took charge of making contacts in her new community and developing a social life that did not depend solely upon that of her daughter.

Change of Scene

Every home I've occupied—with and without a husband and children—has had special charms. I've owned and rented apartments. I've lived in two rooms in a mansion, had the exclusive use of a "sleeps six" travel trailer, was a temporary increase in available funds since I had decided to lease the home I was leaving as a hedge against changing my mind.

I had made a generous allowance for moving costs and the monthly outlay for the apartment and other expenses at my new location. Within a few months of living on the Central Coast, I was convinced I wanted to remain there. What I did not plan for was the gap in income between the termination of the lease and the sale of the property—my mountain home stood vacant for five months, pending a sale. Costs of ownership (taxes, utilities, assessments) continued.

My adjustment to this problem was to move to a less expensive apartment within the complex I had chosen. Once the property was sold and the funds invested, I recovered most of my losses.

owned and rented houses, a condo, and a mobile home. I've also lived joyfully in campsites beside mountain trails.

When I left the community where my husband died, it was to buy a small resort home with no yard upkeep responsibilities. Neighbors were near and friendly, community activities many, and my surroundings beautiful and restful.

I loved that home, but left it five years later—for several reasons. Though I was as physically fit as most of my children, they complained that I was too far away from them. If I were to have an accident or health problems, no child had the resources or the time to tend Mom on her remote mountaintop.

Another reason, the one that sealed the decision, was the experience of helping my cousins move their mother, my ninety-eight-year-old aunt, into a care facility. It was heartbreaking for all of us. Auntie did not want to leave her home of forty years, a nest feathered with curiously preserved junk mail, teetering stacks of precious mementos, and boxes of unidentified photographs.

I was happy to help, but wading through her flotsam—what to save, throw out, or give away—convinced me that I didn't want to put my eight children through such an exercise. I decided to do my own throwaway long before I reached 100.

I sold that precious home and moved to a totally different environment a dozen miles from the Pacific. This location put me within easy reach of—but not on the doorsteps of—all offspring and resulted in joyful experiences different from anything I'd ever known—including a one-season-fits-all climate.

Financial Considerations

Often, due to fixed incomes or other factors, the ability to live for less in another place lures us to move. Or, it might be that selling our current abode and investing the proceeds would provide extra cash for day-to-day living.

The "Should You Move?" Checklist

Only you can assess the lures and challenges of a move. To help you review your needs and wants, a few questions are listed here for your consideration.

Divide a large sheet of paper into three columns. Write the questions below and others you come up with in the left column. Title the other two columns "Pro" and "Con."

Write answers to your questions in the appropriate Pro and Con columns. Once this is completed in your own words, the move may appear different from when all the pros and cons were battling each other inside your head.

- Why do you want to move? House too large, too small, too expensive; climate too severe; emotional ties too depressing or too binding. (Do not make a decision based purely on the loss of a loved one or on the sudden departure of a child or other relative.)
- What are the financial considerations? (Have you anticipated all of them?)
- Are you willing to give up a familiar church, established friends, your hairdresser or barber?
- Does your HMO service the new destination? Are you willing to change medical or dental services?
- Will your auto insurance costs increase, diminish?
- Do you want to live nearer to (or father away from) close relatives?
- Do you want to keep your car or depend on public transportation? (Are you a confident driver and able to drive comfortably alone, knowledgeable about maps and finding routes? Can you afford, and is it possible to use, a golf-cart or a bicycle in your new town? Are train, bus, air transport available so you can visit the place you are leaving or other desired destinations?)

- Are you willing to risk making a mistake or two
  as you adapt to a new location?

Testing The List

You may want to show your list of questions and your answers to an objective associate, one who has *your* best interests at heart. This will not be your dearest friend who can't endure your leaving his or her area. It will not be a real estate agent who might like to handle the sale of your property. It will not be the devoted child who now lives nearest you and doesn't want any changes in distance for visits. Your minister will sympathize but won't want to lose you as a parishioner. The best help may come from the chairman of your nearby American Association of Retired Persons or a professional consultant.

By the time you have reviewed your list, you should be able to make the decision. In the final analysis, the decision has to be yours. If all systems are "go," you have met the challenge and are ready to tackle a "moving adventure."

Where to move to? is the question treated in the next chapter.

2

Location, Location, Location

$\mathbf{Y}$ou have completed your checklist from Chapter 1 and tallied the pros and cons. The conclusion may be a surprise: You absolutely *don't want to and don't have to move*. In that case, put this book away—but don't throw it away. In this unpredictable life, you may need it later.

If your list indicates that a move is inevitable, advantageous, or desirable, your next most important task is attitude adjustment. For some, this will take a shot of bourbon, for others a bowl of chicken soup—or maybe several of each. Anxiety and vacillation will hamper progress toward the Big Event. That, of course, is what every move is—a huge undertaking. However, once the decision is made, the way is cleared for action. Be prepared for shooting the rapids or becoming becalmed to the point of frustration, but these are equally important learning processes on the path to making this the greatest—but not necessarily the last—moving adventure yet. Welcoming the move adds challenge, momentum, and informative surprises.

What? You don't like surprises? Then do not move. Stay where you are and wonder for the rest of your days what your future might have been if you had gathered your courage, donned a fresh sense of adventure, and vaulted into a new life.

List Those Needs

We who look forward to living the better half of our lives in a new location seek places that provide—among other things—a pleasant climate, blood pressure-compatible elevations, adequate medical services, and accessible cultural and recreational opportunities.

I'm an advocate of lists. They help us visualize and organize the tasks at hand. Use the information below to start, but be sure to customize your lists for your own particular wants and needs.

The DDS, MD & HMO Concerns

Preserving our life's adventure certainly gives health care priority. If you are rugged enough to spend the balance of your years in a mountain cabin at 5,000-foot elevation, eating wild mushrooms and venison, go for it. My dear friend Henry is one of these types and something of a recluse. He's determined to stick it out in the surroundings he loves, regardless of the possibility of health emergencies.

Those who have had long careers with industrial, educational or service organizations may have continuing health insurance as part of retirement benefits. My first acquaintance with Kaiser Health Insurance was through my husband's employment at Kaiser Aerospace & Electronics in Southern California. We were pleased with the plan and kept it for the whole family following his retirement. By the end of his life, he had been served with thousands of dollars worth of excellent care, including several surgeries. As a result of this affiliation I was on the Kaiser health care rolls in three different California counties. To my dismay, the Kaiser HMO did not (and still does not, as of this writing) serve residents of my next chosen destination, the Central Coast of California. I did find satisfactory service here. But, in my opinion, it is not as good as my original health plan. Had I been chronically ill or in need of major surgery, I probably would have remained within the Kaiser care network.

Personal Visit

As you ponder the move and consider where to locate, you may recall from earlier days a community or region of ideal climate and beauty. Is it the charming village you and your spouse visited in the '70s and decided was the perfect retirement destination? Be sure to check it out. You can evaluate it from a distance through the library, mailed inquiries or the Internet, but a personal visit is much better.

We are warned to read between the lines in written documents. Please also read between the borders of those magnificent photographs in promotional literature. Do you believe that the four-color booklets touting Florida sanctuaries for seniors are going to include pictures of a hurricane-ravaged shore? Or will California brochures show pictures of the Coalinga collapse in the quake of '82? It's your job to investigate all variations in climate and the frequency of natural disasters particular to a prospective location.

Given possible energy shortages and rolling blackouts, are you physically and emotionally equipped to weather severe heat or severe cold, annual floods or periodic droughts?

Check Out the Chamber

The most thorough test of the location is to spend at least a day or two in an area during its worst time of year weather-wise, as well as its best, if you can manage to do so. Visit that remembered dream area and any other location that appealed to you in the past or has sparked your interest during your current research.

Even if you are website-savvy, neither the Web nor brochures will give you all the information you need. Major help will come from local chambers of commerce. "The customer is always right" is a slogan branded into the minds of most chamber employees and they will not consider you a pest if you pepper them with questions. They have information on such resources as local transportation, churches, adult education classes, art galleries, libraries and parks.

For further information, the chamber clerk will direct you to such senior-specific organizations as the RSVP (Retired Senior and Volunteer Program). Another helpful source is the federally-funded Area Agency on Aging. (I've suggested the name be changed to *Area Agency on Advancement* but am not likely to get this adopted soon.) The chamber office can also direct you to senior centers and the offices of American Association of Retired Persons. Welcome Wagon is another resource. (See the "Resources" section for contact information.)

If you fear that senior-oriented groups will seek to prop you up in a padded rocking chair on the front porch of retirement, think again. They will offer more activities than you want or need. Most members of the SLO-Pokes branch of the San Luis Obispo Bicycle Club, for instance, are fifty-five or over. They schedule weekly group rides. One member is welcomed with her three-wheel bike.

The Senior Saunterers meet weekly for a moderate walk or hike in nearby hills. The Audubon Society and the Sierra Club schedule bird watching and hiking for all ages.

VolksWalkers branches span the globe (See "Resources" for the American Volkssport Association). Originated in Germany after World War II, the organization has taken root in the United States and its activity programs are rapidly gaining widespread popularity. Local leaders schedule walks of all degrees of difficulty and encourage companionable strolling.

Money Counts

Compare costs in the new location with those in the area you are leaving. Rental rates and property costs, food and restaurant prices, movies, auto maintenance, utilities, and public transportation may vary significantly from what you have known at your current home.

You may also want a list of motel prices for use of visiting relatives and friends, and public storage facilities in the event you need space for furnishings you can't part with.

Some of this data can be provided by the local chamber of commerce, other gathered on the Internet or from friends who already live there, but my advice is to visit the prospective location if at all possible and do your own research first hand.

"As Ye Sow..."

Whatever your hobbies or interests, you should be able to find an outlet for them in virtually any community you join. One of my favorite examples is Amy, age ninety. Her education and career experiences were in business and she also mothered two offspring, now long grown and gone. She is not a trained teacher but loves children. She now works three days a week as an aide at an elementary school coaching fourth graders on their written work and arithmetic. She also collects yarn remnants and, during her after-school hours, knits the fragments into colorful afghans and baby sweaters for donation to the local battered women's shelter.

No community in the country is so overloaded with volunteers that it cannot use more. Of course, you are welcome to do nothing but enjoy the parade of sunrises and sunsets if that is your preference for the better half of your life. Just be sure the location you choose has weather patterns that allow such viewing.

Local Newspapers Are Great Resources

When I relocated to the mountain community of Crestline after my husband died, it was my first move as a single woman since leaving home for college. I chose the location for its clear air, redolent with pine, and the pleasant memories it brought of family outings when my children were young.

I knew one person in Crestline, an attorney, who had an office in the village and commuted two days a week to a second office seventy miles distant through Southern California traffic. Though we shared many interests, her time was limited so I could not depend on her for daily chat or counsel.

After unpacking my toothbrush, signing up for a P.O. box, and establishing a check cashing I.D. at the grocery, I picked up my first local reading matter, the weekly newspaper. The *Crestline Courier* was a bonanza of information and gave me a feel for the personality of the community. A single issue listed multiple activities: service club, genealogical and historical group meetings, public events, and yard sales.

It named local environmental and political groups, school events, scheduled hikes, and notices of a dozen different church services. In the "Upcoming Events" column was a listing for the Byliners Writers: "Visitors welcome." From my first attendance at that gathering, my acquaintances and new friends multiplied. Had this not been my special interest, I could have joined the photography group that was compiling a visitors' guide to the area's wildflowers. Mentoring children at the public school was a need. Meals on Wheels sought drivers and the Arboretum needed staff for its information booth. Even though I moved from that precious mountain home in Crestline after five years, I still keep in frequent touch with the dear friends I made there.

Location Choices that Won and Lost

Choosing a location is closely tied to your individual preferences, so it is impossible to advise specifically. However here are examples of a few "better-half seekers" who have the gumption and enthusiasm to keep on moving in order to get it just right.

Be Friendly, Meet People

Opportunities to make friends abound, but if you are a little shy, you may be reluctant to reach out. Yet, with just a smidgen of special attention to this, you will discover new friends any and everywhere. For instance you may find that person standing beside you when you linger at the chamber of commerce's brochure rack is also a shy newcomer.

Or strike up a conversation in the grocery checkout line. Most shoppers are delighted to be asked a question they can answer.

Get acquainted with your librarian. She will likely be eager to offer other suggestions for locating groups and events through which you can meet the locals.

As a newcomer to your church, you will be welcomed with invitations to take part in activities in addition to the church service. The right acquaintances and friendships are just around the corner of today but you must turn that corner yourself.

Laverne, a divorced teacher, retired from her position in the Waukegan, Illinois, school system and sold her home there. Her first move (with her precious cat, Miss Kitty) was a small community across the sound from Seattle, Washington. She rented an apartment and established contacts with fellow history buffs and new church friends.

She continued her hobby of sketching which had already provided illustrations for her book on California missions.

However, after five years, she tired of cloudy skies and rain and, to fulfill a lifelong enchantment with aircraft, decided to buy a duplex, then under construction, in Kansas within sight and sound of a military airbase. Though the ambience was her choice, the construction quality of her duplex turned out to be poor and the promised amenities were not in place when she arrived. With the help of an attorney, she is reneging on the sales contract and will soon move to Colorado, not far from the Air Force Academy. Laverne, at seventy-eight, is fortunate to be well enough financed to make such moves without the fear of bankruptcy.

Ada and Glen had lived in Southern California for most of their working lives. Ardent students of Southwest Indian culture, they built, on retirement, a charming pueblo-style home on the outskirts of Santa Fe, New Mexico. Within a year, Ada developed health problems. When they discovered that the desert climate contributed to her repeated illnesses, they sold their unique desert home and returned to the community they had left in California. They purchased another home from which both, now in their late seventies, are retying bonds of friendship and sharing again in community life.

Choices Unlimited

Your choice of location will be influenced by your health, your financial situation, and whether you want to own or rent. The kind of residence you prefer may be a house, an apartment, a mobile home or motor home—even a boat. Or, you may prefer, as one new acquaintance does, a cruise ship. Suzanne simply transfers her gorgeous gowns, jewelry, and travel souvenirs from stateroom to stateroom as she views the world from the decks of luxury liners. (These and other options are reviewed in Chapters 3 and 4.)

Whether your new abode will be humble or majestic, stationary or mobile, isolated or amid the teeming masses, take pleasure in the fact that, as you plan your move, your choices are nearly unlimited and your horizons are, literally, manifold.

Location Checklist

- Nail your needs with heath considerations at the top. Are you willing to change doctors and/or dentists? Does your current HMO service the intended area? Are medical facilities and alternatives that meet your particular needs available in your prospective location?
- Compare the cost of living in the new location with the one you are leaving.
- Visit the new community. Stay long enough to be convinced it is the right choice for you—for now—before you make the final decision.
- Check with the local chamber of commerce about services, recreations, libraries, cultural events, and churches.
- Contact organizations you might like to join and discuss their programs.

3

Finding Satisfactory Shelter

Readers may dream of emulating Suzanne, the peripatetic cruise line resident, and endearing themselves to the management of the world's luxury cruise lines. But her lifestyle—realistically—is open to few of us. For some, simply viewing a heaving ocean brings a like reaction in their stomachs. But not to worry. The choices in housing—on mountain or shore, in city or country—are numerous.

For years I shared with a property-acquisitive husband the opinion that it is foolish to pour money out in monthly rents when mortgage payments can be building equity. Ownership, however, also carries financial and physical responsibilities that can become burdensome. Taxes and maintenance are major costs, in addition to the mortgage. In the mountain community where I lived for five years, for example, I paid assessments to water, sewage, and recreation districts, as well as a fee levied by the school district. I raked leaves and pine needles and shoveled snow in one month or another all year. At the end of those five years, I was convinced I did not want to own a home again—unless it was one on wheels that would serve my wanderlust.

When I calculated the financial as well as physical logistics of moving away from the mountain retreat, I planned that the income I would receive from renting it and later from its sale could be invested to pay me monthly dividends. The theory was sound, but the results did not exactly fit the original plan. Meanwhile, I investigated the many options that lay ahead.

Sampling Through Home Exchange

One way to thoroughly investigate an area is the Senior Home Exchange. It is similar to a time-share but is senior-specific. For a fee, Senior Home Exchange (see "Resources" for contact information) will list your home in an international directory that describes its features and proximity to cultural and recreational opportunities. In this way—without losing your home or actually moving out of it—you may sample another area of the country or the world. Simultaneously, a responsible party will enjoy your home and location for an agreed-upon period of time. Holiswap, based in Australia, offers similar exchanges worldwide.

Another version of home exchange is privately managed. Barbara, a senior in Boulder, Colorado, owns a home there. She extends the pleasure of basic home ownership by using her home to pay for her adventures. She enjoys travel and rents her home through a real estate agent to responsible tenants who enjoy the Colorado winters while Barbara travels and visits her children in Oregon and Southern California. The rent she receives pays her travel expenses and the recreations she enjoys in warmer climes. She visited me at the retirement home where I first lived on the Central Coast.

Barbara says she, too, will eventually move to a retirement complex. She is sixty-five. "However," she says, "I'm enjoying these transition years, combining ownership and escape until—and if—I need to make another choice."

Ownership in Retirement Communities

From Florida to California, builders have created beautiful housing complexes especially designed for super-adults. Condominiums and individual cottages with low-maintenance yards or patios are available. Recreational extras may include golf courses, clubhouses, swimming pools and tennis courts. Whether your preference is the desert or the shore, the North, South, East or West, you may purchase such a home on its own lot and live among others with similar recreational, physical, and social needs. A real estate agent can lead you to such communities, or check the Internet on your own.

Rentals in Retirement Communities

I had no reason to leave my native state of California. It would only add to my children's concerns for me. My primary target was a rental unit of some kind. Renting offers greater flexibility in choices and is ideal—including the renting of a motel room—for sampling a new location. Rentals in retirement communities, as with ownership purchases, are available nationwide. Often, no lease is required. Mature Living Choices (see "Resources") offers regional booklets with listings for independent living in active adult communities, single family homes, and assisted living complexes throughout the United States and in British Columbia, Canada. Books and materials from the library and brochures I'd received in the mail featured retirement rentals in cities from San Diego on the Southern California border to Mount Shasta in the north. The more expensive offered small, individual cottages. Others were multi-apartment structures.

The Central Coast appealed to me largely because it would put me about half way between my children who were living in the northern and southern parts of the state. I drove 300 miles from my mountain home to check out the city of San Luis Obispo. I was fortunate to have one friend in a nearby community. I could bunk with her during my investigation. She knew local highways and business and residential sections and drove me from place to place, speeding my evaluation.

Senior retirement rentals are noted for the many amenities and services they provide. Most of these include a twenty-four-hour staff, meals, and social, recreational, and therapeutic services. A month-to-month contract allows for a change of heart. I visited two retirement apartment facilities within my price range. The first did not appeal to me. I saw only one smiling face—that of the manager.

The second, The Villages, was populated with enthusiastic staff and happily socializing residents. The Villages is comprised of three multiunit complexes at one location and a fourth that specializes in Alzheimer's care. The Palms and The Oaks sections of The Villages are for active seniors. They offer apartments ranging in size from two-bedroom/two bath units with full kitchens to one bedroom/one bath and studio units both with microwave and refrigerator. Gardens and window boxes are filled with lovely flowers, ever-blooming, and tenants need not lift a trowel to keep them that way. The apartments at The Villages are within walking distance of banks, a drugstore, grocery, a dental center and an optometrist. For those who want an occasional change from The Villages dining rooms, a half dozen restaurants are within a few blocks.

Within three days of visiting the community and surroundings, I chose The Palms section for my future home. Even though the corporate van offered transportation, without charge, to any destination in the city limits, I elected to keep my car. I envisioned adventures that would require my own wheels and was gratified to learn that my auto insurance would drop about $200 a year when I moved from the mountain resort to this more heavily-trafficked, but statistically less hazardous location.

Assessment of a new location must include, besides the costs of housing and auto ownership, any significant changes in food prices, utilities, and health maintenance. The monthly fee at The Palms included two daily meals, with a choice of two dinner hours. Beverages, fruit, and snacks were available throughout the day. Gas and electric service were included. Tenants paid for their own telephone and cable TV. I measured the size of each room in the apartment I selected, recording its exact dimensions, the space between windows and doors, and the window heights. This information was for use as I planned what furnishings I would bring to my new home.

When I first told friends I was going to a retirement community, they envisioned me dropping out of circulation into an old folks home. This idea stemmed from the county homes prevalent in the early 1900s where seniors unable to live with their children were warehoused until they obligingly died.

Even with the many advantages of a senior residence facility, some of the better-half-of-lifers object to such housing because all residents are seniors. The crowd at the dining tables presents a sea of gray hair and shining pates. But I discovered an important truth. Many of these heads are filled with fascinating knowledge and their owners generate stimulating conversations—a fact that may be lost on those for whom appearance reigns over brains.

My choice of my future home brought cheers from my children. Although they knew I subscribed to the buddy system for hikes in the mountain area, they had fretted that while living alone there I was likely to fall from my balcony, leave a pot of soup to boil dry, or slip in my bathtub. The first news I sent to the family was the fact that my new home had an emergency call button reachable from the bathtub. Waterproof emergency call pendants are also furnished.

Among the gratifying aspects of The Palms was the presence of the young dining room serving staff, both men and women, most of them part-timers earning their way through one of the two local colleges. Those studying gerontology sought us out for conversation and project reports. However, few acquaintances at the complex yearned for the daily babble of children's voices. Most "loved to have the grandkids come," but were happy that the visits did not extend beyond a couple of days.

Assisted Living

Both The Palms and The Oaks sections of The Villages are dedicated to the comfort and pleasure of independent seniors—those physically and mentally capable of caring for themselves. An additional adjacent complex, Garden Creek, has a full staff of caregivers and nurses to accommodate those with walkers, crutches, or wheelchairs and residents who require medication reminders and assistance in dressing and bathing. Though readers of this book may not require such additional services now, it is important to know that such supplementary help is immediately available. Garden Creek residents take their meals in a gracious dining room, exactly as do those ambulatory residents of The Palms and The Oaks. The cost is significantly higher, reflecting increased services and staffing, but those former residents of the independent living sections who now need extra care retain some of the sense of family they had found during their independent living days next door and can keep in touch with old friends. The availability of such nearby facilities should certainly be investigated when one is considering a retirement home.

Intentional Communities

Although I was happy in my choice of The Palms as my new home, I had investigated several additional options in the process of making a decision. Among these were "intentional communities." Across the country, the concept of planned communities has been in operation since the hippies set out to duplicate Utopia in the '60s. A number of these intentional communities remain in operation, most in rural areas.

Some, like Ananda in Nevada City, California, with branches in Texas and Rhode Island, are centered on mutual religious beliefs.

Fees vary, but all ages are welcomed and nurtured, and all share community responsibilities—both maintenance and governance. Residents do not own their homes but enjoy extended use and choices among various structures. *The Communities Directory: A Guide To Intentional Communities and Cooperative Living* (see "Resources") lists 700 such communities in the United States and Canada.

Another kind of intentional community is for people who seek ownership in an intergenerational community. Tierra Nueva, at Oceano, California, is one among many in which participants purchase homes within a complex dedicated to meeting the needs of all ages. Owners share maintenance and governing responsibilities through committee action.

A concept founded on California's Central Coast, Cut-Rate Cohousing, adapts the strategies and methods of other cohousing methods to existing multifamily facilities—rather than requiring the construction of new units. The plan stresses less expensive collaborative neighborhoods. This program provides the versatility of housing renters or purchasers, seniors or multigenerational residents.

Additional cohousing neighborhoods are springing up throughout the United States and are included among the listings in the *Communities Directory*.

Shared Housing

Sharing living quarters can be tricky. Proof lies in the fact that 50 percent of us seem unable to remain in one marriage for a lifetime. Most better-half-of-lifers—though we are known to argue otherwise—are somewhat set in our ways. Our years of practice have proven to us that our own methods and habits are the most workable ones for us, as individuals. However my *right* may be as *wrong* for a housemate as a loudly playing boom-box would be for me. The originator of the Cut-Rate Cohousing plan, Betty Branch, has published a helpful book, *Housemates' Handbook*, designed specifically for people who are considering sharing financial and household responsibilities under one roof.

Two women I met at The Palms left to try shared housing. Catherine joined her single daughter in the daughter's lovely home. Mother and daughter were not only a generation apart, but each was convinced that the mores of her particular generation were the ones that should be in practice in the shared household. "It was best for peace among all my kids that I return to The Palms," says Catherine.

Georgia moved into the home of a lifelong friend. This was intended to provided companionship and reduce expenses for both. "We discovered we do not like the same foods, and it was uncomfortable and wasteful trying to prepare two different dinners side by side. Even though I paid rent, I always felt I had to ask permission to use the laundry and the oven." When Georgia decided that the independence she enjoyed at The Palms was worth the extra cost, she moved back. "We're still good friends, but would not have been if I remained in her home."

My Current Choice

Shared housing is the choice that has brought me—and *one* pickup load of belongings—to the home I now occupy.

One afternoon late in 1991, I answered the phone. "How

about the Galapagos?" came the excited question from a voice I recognized immediately. It was Allison, newly-retired teacher, mother of grown children and, most important, a friend of the wherever-and-all-ways sort. Throughout a long acquaintance we had shared children's accomplishments and woes, their weddings, divorces, births of grandchildren, and the heartbreaks and loss of dear colleagues. We had spoken often of taking an overseas trip together.

The sudden loss of my husband six months earlier had left me with questions about my future and where I wanted to settle. Allison, also single, was considering a move away from our community. We both felt that a change of scene and an exotic adventure would bring perspective to our lives. We were eligible for an Elderhostel trip, and I agreed that the unique and magnificent Galapagos was a perfect destination.

For many years Allison had owned a small home on California's Central Coast. It had been a base for several of her children who attended colleges in the area. Later, it became an income-producing rental. By the time we returned from the Galapagos adventure, she was ready to move back into her Central Coast home. I, too, was ready to sell my home in the town where we met. I chose the San Bernardino mountains of California. We visited often, taking pleasure in showing off the beauties of our distinctive locations. When I decided that my mountain retreat was too challenging in climate and too remote for easy access to my children, I moved to the Central Coast, first to The Palms, then to home-sitting for a friend, before moving on to a private apartment.

Allison and I had long considered that in our old age—
"well past sixty," then "well past seventy"—we would
weigh the values of living under the same roof. Close proximity would mean simplified planning for more travel, the
pleasure of companionship, and the mutual assistance that
is often needed in our later years.

To shorten my account of my moving adventures, the
happy resolution is that my final (?) move has brought me
to Allison's lovely home. I pay a rental fee that helps her
enhance the home's décor and expand the garden she loves.
Dividing expenses and responsibilities makes more funds
available for our travels.

It is assumed that any two friends considering life as
owner and renter under the same roof have already tested
their compatibility in enough different circumstances that
the personal habits of each are known and mutually acceptable. Allison and I have met the trials of constant togetherness required in the sardine packing of airline seats. We have
searched for contact lenses by flashlight on the rolling floor
of a ship's cabin and clung together as we faced the muzzle
of a handgun upon the late arrival at the home of a friend.

As all married couples and others who own a home
together know, give-and-take is the primary rule. Additional
rules apply when one is the owner and the other a tenant.
The workability of sharing a common roof varies with the
relative importance of the timing of daily routines and individual schedules, finances, companionship, and security.

Maintaining Independence While Sharing

My housemate Allison and I have many friends and

activities in common and many we enjoy separately. She keeps in daily contact with her children and twelve grand-children by telephone and e-mail. My children, though loving and supportive, are not as social, and they have produced only three grandchildren. As a result, our family-related activities vary considerably.

Allison and I have separate automobiles and telephone services. Each of us has our own computer, radio, and television set.

I clean my own room and bath and help wherever needed with other housekeeping and maintenance chores. I care for her pets and the house and garden when she goes out of town, and I am free to leave for visits with friends and family, confident that my possessions are safe.

When we are away from home on separate occasions, we don't have to arrange with the post office to hold mail, stop the paper delivery or have a neighbor set out the containers for refuse collection.

Allison graciously insists that I consider the home mine. The guestroom has housed my visitors as well as hers. Some days we are so engrossed in our separate endeavors we see little of each other.

So far, we have not encountered the problems met by Georgia, my acquaintance who left The Palms to live with a friend but returned to the complex because she was uncomfortable sharing the facilities of a home owned by another.

My work at the computer keeps me alone in my room for many hours. Allison writes, paints, does freelance editing and tutoring. She loves to cook and prepares the dinners. I do the dishes. We're on our own for breakfasts and lunches. We walk daily but rarely together as the timing and distances we prefer are not the same, but we do plan special weekend hikes to scenic vistas with mutual friends. In other words, each of us lives alone—but we do it together.

Shared Rentals

A better way, perhaps, to share a home with a friend or relative is to rent a structure for which you share equally in rental fees, upkeep, and utilities. This removes any sense of priority that is bound to be a part of the equation when one partner is the sole owner. If Georgia had shared a rental unit with her friend rather than occupying a part of her friend's home, their living together might have been successful.

Shared Housing: Family

Catherine and Georgia notwithstanding, shared housing—whether with a spouse, other relative, or friend—can be a very practical solution and should not be discounted. Adele is a good example. Her son and his wife hold full-time jobs. They have a five-year-old daughter. After her husband died, Adele (then sixty) went to live temporarily at the son's home until she got her bearings.

She bonded quickly with the grandchild, Sally. After a few weeks, the young couple offered Adele the opportunity to share their home in exchange for caring for Sally. With the child in preschool, Adele spends her mornings alone but picks up the granddaughter each day. She is free to participate in community activities in the evenings. Grandmother and Sally are happy companions.

Adele has her own bedroom and bath, but the rest of the quarters are shared. She grocery shops and prepares evening meals as her contribution to the costs of the rented home.

"We have minor conflicts," Adele says, "but the arrangement is so beneficial to all of us, we just attribute any differences to the fact that each is a strong personality, and we don't try to change each other."

Another example of family-shared housing is a part of my experience. During the mid-'70s when we lived in the mobile home on our mini-ranch, my sister, her husband, and three children came to live with us.

Our location was about halfway between Los Angeles and San Francisco, giving my brother-in-law a midpoint for exploring employment opportunities in both metropolitan centers. We housed them in one of the three bedrooms in our mobile home, and in our on-premises travel trailer.

They had exclusive use of one bathroom in the mobile home. We ate meals together, dividing the cost. They helped tend our livestock and garden and their willingness to manage ranch chores allowed my husband and me to take our first vacation in five years.

This family grouping ended after eight months when our visitors relocated with the aerospace industry to Northern California. The shared housing arrangement had been consistently amicable and is a treasured memory for us all. One important element in this experience was that we knew from the outset that the situation would be temporary.

Families sharing premises do not always find it so jolly. Two favorite characters I met during my mountain days were a midaged daughter and her elderly mother who had lived together for twenty years.

Perpetual disagreement was the theme of their lives. Among their daily confrontations was temperature regulation. For one, the house was always too hot. For the other, it was too cold. The carpet in front of their wall thermostat was threadbare from the steady traffic.

Shared Housing: Owner/Tenant

After purchasing my mountain cottage, I invested enough in remodeling to create a studio apartment in its basement. This addition increased the value of the home and was a source of income. The unit had a separate entrance and I rented it to a series of single, employed adults for as long as I owned the property.

The arrangement was completely businesslike and the main contacts were made on rent-due days and to keep each other informed of planned absences. My children endorsed this arrangement, feeling that simply having another body on the property was a kind of security they could not provide because of their great distance from me.

Shared Housing: Owner/Tenant/Companion

Gloria, owner of a comfortable three-bedroom home was lonely after her last child left to pursue a career elsewhere. She advertised a room for rent with kitchen privileges on the bulletin board of the local community college and gained a roomer who became an ideal tenant, not unlike a member of the family.

When this girl left the community for a four-year college, Gloria advertised again and got a second, excellent tenant, friendly and responsible. This girl remained for more than a year until she married.

In these instances, the tenants provided Gloria with extra income, companionship, and the security of an extra pair of eyes and ears on the property.

The third time for Gloria was not so charming. The tenant was not employed and spent most of every day in Gloria's kitchen engaged in creative cooking—and eating. This was more togetherness than Gloria needed or wanted. That fiasco ended when Gloria sold the property and moved to another community.

Shared Housing: Paid Companion

It sometimes becomes necessary for reasons of chronic health problems to hire a live-in companion to monitor medications, prepare food and do housekeeping. The situation is common among seniors who elect to remain in their own homes rather than move into a commercial, assisted living situation. It is of vital importance that the individual employed be compatible, have good references, and keep the interests and needs of the homeowner foremost in his or her mind.

Emergency Concerns

Each domestic partner should know the wishes of the other in case of illness or accident. Both should know location of important papers, whom to notify, and under what conditions life support and other emergency measures are desired. Both should make wishes known to heirs, and both should notify these heirs that they have instructed their domestic partner on how to meet any emergency that affects one partner or the other.

Resolution of Differences

Set an annual or six-month capability review schedule, but agree in advance that all intermittent disagreements be brought up for discussion at once.

Checklist of Guidelines for Sharing a Home

Shared housing will last only as long as it is comfortable and mutually supportive and honors the interests and needs of all parties. The first item on the list of agreements for Allison and me is that the arrangement does not have to be permanent.

Here are a few additional concepts that guide us. It may not be necessary to formalize your list with a signed contract, but each factor should be discussed when one roof is to shelter such domestic partners as owner and tenant-friend.

- Agree on a rental fee and recognize that it may need to change as costs inevitably rise.
- What is covered in the fee? (Utilities, parking, storage, food?)
- Agree on when the rental fee is due.
- What space is to be occupied by tenant as his or her private domain?
- Are kitchen and laundry privileges included?

Money Matters

Happy as I was at The Palms, I left there after two years. My next move was necessary for financial reasons. In January we were given written notice that the first of March would bring a significant raise in monthly fees.

I could have covered the amount—at least for that year—but the cushion between my fixed income and fixed outlay would be so flattened it would leave me little extra for fun—and the fees certainly weren't slated to go down in the foreseeable future.

From the county Area Agency on Aging, I got a list of complexes that offered independent living similar to The Villages. I was disheartened to discover that the charges for all were about the same—or higher—than I was then paying.

One complex, Temple Escape, however, was one I could afford. It was set in a groomed courtyard of individual apartments and rented to seniors only.

- For mutual benefit, is the tenant-occupied space away from the main avenues of traffic through the home?
- Are there limits on use of the rented space? Consider such things as picture-hanging and other alterations of the décor.
- Consider the noise-level tolerance of both. Will two TVs conflict for the listening pleasure of each? (Ear phones can be purchased and plugged

Temple had a small recreation room with a kitchen. Those who wished were encouraged to shop and prepare meals together. But each unit had its own kitchen as well. It was soon to have a vacancy and offered the independence I sought.

Temple was perfect for me, but there was a catch. Living there would put me twenty-five miles from the community of friends and activities I had established during my two years at The Palms. To keep up the contacts I enjoyed, I'd have to spend too much time commuting and the route was an always-busy freeway. I put Temple Escape on hold as I explored further.

Rentals of all sizes from rooms to large homes are available in most communities and the classified section of the newspaper is the best source of information. Even though such a place would not give me an emergency call button or waiter-served meals I decided that my next abode would be a small rental apartment where I would prepare my own meals and pay my own utilities.

into the TV to adjust the sound level appropriately for a hearing-impaired listener.)

- What will be the maintenance responsibilities for each, including dish washing and general cleaning?
- What items are to be shared? Consider things like refrigerator space, laundry, TV, VCR, phone service, and newspapers. If one TV must be shared, how important are specific programs to each?

- Is smoking by tenant or guests allowed? Is liquor permitted?
- Consider all health conditions: dietary limitations, allergies, hearing impairments. Are there current or anticipated problems with access—steps, ramps, inside stairways?
- What are the rules for pets if either sharing partner is to have one or more?
- For those with different ambient temperature preferences, is individual space heating possible or allowable?
- Consider visits of guests and children. Does either frown upon unmarried guests occupying the same bed?

House-Sitting

Another acquaintance at The Palms, Marilyn, had an opportunity to house-sit for the daughter of a long-term friend. The daughter, Sandra, was single and employed in a distant city. She loved her home on the Central Coast where she kept pets and a garden but could spend only long weekends there. When her mother proposed that the two get together, the two generations hit it off and Marilyn rented the spare bedroom in Sandra's lovely home. This reduced Marilyn's monthly costs and provided surveillance for Sandra's expensive property as well as care of her pets. Such opportunities are available to responsible seniors. Word of mouth is probably the best method of contact, though the classified sections of newspapers often show such listings.

Federally Subsidized Housing

The U.S. Department of Housing and Urban Development (HUD) subsidizes housing for seniors whose incomes are insufficient to cover rental and living costs in their communities. One fellow senior, whom I met through a local art appreciation group, had found such an apartment and was very satisfied with it. She told me about Autumn Leaves, another HUD complex. I toured the facility, very much like The Villages, though not as large. The gracious manager gave me an application form and told me there was at least a one-year waiting list. "However," she assured me, "you never know when the apartment you want will become available."

Even if the wait were a year, I could manage in my Palms quarters if I cut back on lunches out with friends, shared a newspaper subscription with my neighbor, and used the library for magazines instead of renewing subscriptions. If the kids wanted me to come for Christmas, they could help foot the transport bill.

Delighted with the possibility of joining the Autumn Leaves community, I filled out the detailed application.

Within two days, the director called me for a repeat interview. She had some reservations. The problem: My income from Social Security, a small widow's pension and a few dividends put me on the cusp of eligibility for HUD housing. I was okay now but if I earned any substantial funds from my writing hobby (a lifelong enthusiasm that has netted me more pleasure than dollars), I would exceed the income allowable for residents of Autumn Leaves.

Like all writers, I always hope for a big slice of that pie in the sky. If the hoped-for largess came, I didn't want it to put me out on the street. Even with my practice in moving, I don't want to do it more times than necessary.

Let Your Needs Be Known

Volunteering in the community had brought new friends. One of my projects was minor clerical work at the Women's Community Center. As the monthly board meeting broke up, I asked if anyone knew of a small apartment that was available for rent. Most of the group, all younger than I, shook their heads, but the day's chairperson said, "My landlady is looking for a mature woman who doesn't mind climbing steps."

As a lifelong hiker, I welcomed any extra exercise and walked the two blocks from our meeting place to present myself to the landlady. She found me mature (of course) and led me up the slope and then up two flights of steps. She apparently concluded I was sufficiently agile to manage in the one-bedroom rental. The price was right—far less than I was currently paying at The Palms.

She did not require a long-term lease and was willing to sign me up. In my initial survey, I discovered that the plumbing was nearly my age, but operational. The view from her hilltop was a lovely panorama of steeple tops and green hills, and the location was within walking distance of the library and shopping of all kinds.

I was lucky, but I've found that good luck has a habit of finding those who maintain an attitude that expects it. I measured the new apartment and sketched in the location of the doors and windows so that I could decide on the arrangement of furniture in advance.

The few pieces I had kept since significantly reducing their number in prior moves were exactly right for this apartment. A discount mover whose truck was a direct descendant of the vehicle that brought the Joads from Oklahoma carried my possessions to my new digs in one load.

Checklist of Options

Below is a summary of housing options and the experiences described in the above chapter. Contact information for named resources and organizations is listed alphabetically in the "Resources" section.

• Home Exchange: Contract will provide details of what you can expect and what is expected of you.

• Purchase in a Retirement Community: You own your own property but are subject to the rules of the community's residents' association.

• Renting in a Senior Retirement Community: Ask about the amenities available at each senior retirement home. Compare the offerings of several.

• Assisted Living Homes: Check the availability of this service in the vicinity of the new home you choose.

• Intentional Communities: See the directory listed in Resources.

• Collaborative Rental Communities: Contact manager. (See Resources.)

• Shared Housing: Owner/Family; Owner/Tenant; Owner/Tenant/Companion; Paid Companion, House-Sitting: Weigh the advantages and disadvantages of each of these housing options before making a final decision.

- Federally Subsidized Housing: Contact the Area Agency on Aging in the county you are investigating.
- Independent Rentals: Per contract with landlord.

4

A Moveable Feast of Choices

So you have decided to sell the old homestead or the palatial condo or end your rental agreement and move on. You have investigated and visited several locations which meet your health needs and are tempting for climate, recreational, and cultural opportunities—as well as being affordable. However, you're not 100 percent convinced which one is the perfect location in which to plant your "new roots." The good news is that you can sample areas and "moving" life styles for extended periods of time without making an *absolutely final* choice. Perhaps you may even elect to sample a floating home.

Mobile Homes

Location sampling can be accomplished in several ways. A house that can be moved from place to place is a possibility. Mobile homes, though moved on wheels from place to place, do not retain their wheels. They are ideal for many seniors, partnered or single.

The homes range in size from a single-wide unit (roughly 12' x 50') with bedroom, living space, kitchen, and bath to a double-wide, (24' x 50' or more) with up to three bedrooms, two baths, and as much luxury as you are willing to purchase.

Most mobile homes are less expensive in initial cost than a wood and masonry structure. When set up and groomed for the location these can be as comfortable and as attractive as a house with a traditional foundation.

Those who expect to move from area to area often purchase mobile homes and have them installed on leased or rented ground. Sewer, electric, and gas connections must be available on the property.

Insurance costs vary, but in earthquake and tornado-prone areas, premiums are high.

Moving a mobile home is somewhat expensive. It involves hiring trucks and their drivers who specialize in this kind of transport. But, when you consider that the furniture and other contents can remain in place (strapped down, boxed, and balanced by the movers) during the move, for those who like plenty of living space, privacy, and storage, this may be the most economical way to roam periodically. (For an example, see Chapter 5, "Memorable Moves.")

Mobile Home Parks

Local zoning laws will apply but mobile homes can be set up on almost any lot. Mobile home parks, however, have many advantages. The parks range in accommodations from the minimal service parks that also allow travel trailers to beautifully landscaped areas with paved streets, sewer, gas, and electric hookups similar to any housing development. The homes are set on roughly equal-size lots with individual street addresses. Some offer small gardening spaces and carports. A central laundry room, a swimming pool, and one or more recreation halls provide space for meetings, crafts, dinners, dances, and other entertainment. Luxury parks may provide a nine-hole golf course, tennis and shuffleboard courts, and swimming pools.

Tenants of the park own their mobile homes but pay a fixed monthly rental fee for their spaces and for some utilities, such as phone and cable TV. A more recent option in some mobile home parks is group ownership of the property by the residents—usually via a corporation—with individual ownership of the homes. Corporation members hold annual budget meetings to determine the fees for occupancy and grounds maintenance.

Those who move from a home on a traditional-sized lot may be stressed at first by the nearness of neighbors whose exterior walls, in many cases, are within eight to a dozen feet away. On the other hand, this proximity provides near-perfect security and a kind of helpful surveillance. Neighbors soon learn each other's habits and movements and check if illness or accident is suspected.

For George and Kate, living in a mobile home park was ideal until his hearing loss became so great and the volume of his daily TV so loud that neighbors complained. Until then, neither George nor Kate had known that earphones could be plugged into the TV, with the sound adjusted to individual hearing needs. The couple made the earphones purchase on the recommendation of the park manager. The earphones brought the required volume to George's ears while Kate listened at normal volume, and the neighborhood returned to peaceful coexistence.

Some mobile home parks restrict their tenants to adults only, seniors only, or maintain both family and senior sections. Check with the management regarding any immediate or future plans to accept families that include young children or teenagers.

If you are not enthusiastic about intergenerational neighborhoods, you will want to learn whether the park offers separate sections for families and seniors and whether these sections are separated by sound barriers.

Further, when considering a mobile home park, check out the space pricing history. Preferably, talk with a long-term resident in the park and with the park's membership association. In some parks, space rental goes up every several years in small increments. In others, sale of the park property may result in a substantial rise in space costs.

Seasonal Snowbirds

Millie and Mike, seventy and eighty-five, own a traditional home on a spacious lot in Bend, Oregon. Every fall, they travel in their car a thousand miles to California's Imperial Valley to winter in their second home, a fully equipped and furnished double-wide mobile home in a large park, the Fountain of Youth Spa and Recreational Vehicle Resort. Early in the summer, they reverse their path, driving home to their other roots in Oregon.

The Imperial Valley resort offers therapeutic mineral baths, a general store, laundries, swimming pools, four recreation halls, and a putting green, to mention only a few of the amenities.

The nearby Salton Sea, California's largest lake, offers

A Million RVers Can't All Be Wrong

In addition to structures rooted in the earth, recreational vehicles by the thousands carry superadults from climate to climate and from one scenic location to another.

On one trip through the West by car I conducted an informal survey of RVs on the road compared to the number of passenger vehicles. While this was in the summer time when lots of recreational traffic is expected, I was surprised to find the numbers to be near fifty-fifty.

I doubt that all the RVers were in the better half of their lives, but all were keeping their lives exciting and adventurous.

---

boating, fishing, and water sports. Some owner-tenants—both singles and couples—live year-round at this park, which boasts space for 800 mobile homes. Another 200 spaces accommodate transient visitors who drop in for a weekend or more in their recreational vehicles.

Year-round Snowbirds

Millie and Mike are one kind of snowbird. Others of this growing "flock" travel constantly in their RVs. These may be a self-propelled motor home, a fifth wheel which is a combination of tow-vehicle and living quarters, or a travel trailer that is towed either by a passenger car or truck.

Their owners take advantage of ideal climates and scenic venues in national parks and at festivals and cultural activities across the country. Owners with unlimited resources may ship their motorized vehicles abroad for similar touring.

Such houses on wheels are ideal for couples or partners researching the ideal place to settle or for those whose wanderlust inclinations keep them moving. Turtle-like, their homes are always on their backs. Mobile home parks for transient and long-term renting are listed in every telephone directory in the country.

The requirements of driving and vehicle maintenance are not always easily shouldered by a single person. However, testimony to the appeal of RVing for all situations is the fact that Loners On Wheels, a singles RV group, has been in existence for more than thirty years.

The *KOA Kampgrounds Directory* provides maps and specific locations of its campgrounds—available for tent campers and RVers alike—in every state in the union, in Mexico, and Canada. Convenience stores, swimming pools and laundry facilities are available in most.

Some KOAs offer small log cabins (Kamping Kottages) with shower, kitchenette, and sleeping quarters for up to four people.

Motor Home

A motor home (one of three major types of RVs), unlike a mobile home, is a single unit on permanent wheels with the piloting portion fully accessible to the living portion.

One partner can leave the copilot seat for a bathroom

break or to prepare lunch in the compact kitchen while the other drives along the highway. When one tires of driving, he or she can take a nap on the bed while the other steers the unit along the highway.

These large vehicles get eight to ten miles to a gallon of gasoline. Some are diesel powered. To save fuel in the big rig and increase mobility at a campsite, owners often tow a compact car or pull a small trailer that carries a motorcycle or golf cart behind the motor home.

These small, more economical vehicles are used to commute to the grocery store or to run other errands while the motor home is parked at the campsite.

Travelers who enjoy fishing or boating often mount canoes or kayaks atop their RVs.

Fifth Wheel

A fifth wheel is similar to a motor home but it is a style of trailer that is towed by a pickup truck. The "fifth" wheel is a term derived from the disk to which the trailer is attached on the truck bed. It allows the trailer section pivoting flexibility as it is being towed.

Access to the living space of a fifth wheel is not possible from the cab of the truck. However, like motor homes, these trailers can be as elaborate as funds allow.

The sleeping section of the fifth wheel normally extends over the truck bed and requires an inside ladder for access, an important consideration for the less agile. (Some motor homes also require climbing a ladder to reach the sleeping quarters.)

The significant advantage of the fifth wheel is that once

the living portion is parked and its cab-over section supported on built-in stilts, the truck can be used for commuting to and from the campsite for groceries and other errands.

Travel Trailer

A conventional travel trailer—the granddaddy of all RVs—depending on its size, may be towed by a passenger car, truck or van. Modern trailers, as with motor homes and fifth wheels, are equipped with living area, kitchen, bed and bathroom with shower. All are remarkable examples of space economy. Every square inch is pressed into service for living or storage. The major disadvantage with a trailer is that most states do not allow passengers to ride in the trailer while the rig is on the road. For couples who share the driving on long hauls, this can be a disadvantage in that anyone wanting to snooze can't do so until the unit is parked.

Many of today's trailers and fifth wheels feature a slide-out, sometimes called a pop-out. This is a room (one or more) with walls and floors that telescope in and out of the main unit. The pop-out slides out to add space when the vehicle is parked.

Whether the home on wheels is a motor home, a fifth wheel or a trailer, the advantages for retirees are many. If they don't like the scenery or sociability of a location, they can move on in a matter of minutes, carrying their worldly goods and personal interests to a new park or highway viewpoint. A recently inaugurated adventure for RVers is the trip aboard a train's flat car, traveling at a scenery-enhancing speed along the rim of Mexico's magnificent Copper Canyon.

The social community built by these nomads is strong and rewarding. "We have the best of all worlds," report Margaret and Fred, motor home owners. "We meet new people all the time, so we can tell and retell our favorite stories without boring the listeners."

Bob and Beatrice have combined some of the best aspects of wheeled versatility. They purchased a twenty-eight-foot travel trailer on their retirement in 1990, planning to tour the country for three months. They put their college-aged daughter in charge of their permanent home on a pleasant tree-sheltered street in Logan, Utah. The planned three-month tour turned into eight years of touring the country from Maine to Mexico, Alaska to Florida. After this much travel, they returned to Logan. The daughter had married and given birth to two children. She and her husband were ready to purchase their own home. Bob and Bea, by then in their late seventies and sated with traveling, settled back into their permanent home in Logan.

Monthly RV magazines and web sites devoted to RV life compare vehicles and new equipment, list RV rally locations, and provide information on major RV shows throughout the country. You can visit these to inspect and evaluate what kind is best for you.

Dock It

Another "moving" example of retirement pleasure comes from Alice. She and Andy, then in their late fifties, moored their small boat in a slip at Pismo Beach, California. Their land transportation was a camper, an early version of a motor home. (A camper is a small living unit mounted in the bed of a pickup truck.) They parked it at dockside and used it as living quarters when they traveled on land and to supply shoreside needs. The boat, complete with galley, sanitary facilities, and beds, served as primary housing. They lived on their boat, *Sweet & Low*, in both California and Florida for five years in the first location and for three in the second. Their combined sea and shore life was "economical and fun," says Alice.

They took the boat into various bays and along coastal waters to explore and fish. "We ate a lot of seafood and about the only arguments we had were over whose turn it was to clean the catch."

After Andy's death, Alice sold the camper and the boat and is happily settled in another kind of shared housing back in California.

In his 1993 book, *Maybe (Maybe Not)*, Robert Fulgham, now in his sixties, reports that he and his wife have lived on a houseboat for several years. He refers to it as an "aquatic trailer court" and says that he likes living up close to those who live around him. "I compare my life to theirs. I learn from them and am enriched by gifts they never realize they give."

Workers on Wheels

From Illahee State Park near Bremerton, Washington, Will and Sue write: "We sold our home in 1998, acquired an RV and went looking for a place to volunteer as hosts. We found that parks in every state are actively recruiting volunteer help. This includes county, state, and national parks, forest services, the National Bureau of Land Management, Army Corps of Engineers, and probably other agencies we have not heard of. We spend summers in the Northwest and winter months in Arizona. Last winter we were at San Rafael Ranch, a new state park located on the border with Mexico. We will be returning there this winter where we are helping to restore this historic ranch. For those who wish to earn a salary, many agencies hire seasonal employees as do privately owned RV parks."

Workamper News, a bimonthly newsletter, lists jobs available at campgrounds and resorts. *Full-Time RVing* is a book filled with information for all RVers or for those considering enjoying RV life while earning part of their travel expenses.

Volunteers are normally provided space for their RV. Water, electricity, and sewer are also usually provided and, in some places, so is a telephone. Volunteers serve as the eyes and ears of the campground, helping to clean it, answering questions, and reminding campers of the rules. They put in about twenty hours a week. "We look at each park as another part of our adventure in life," says Will.

Workers at Sea

People who enjoy working with others; retirees with skills and experience in hospitality, entertainment, fitness, health care; and former teachers may wish to contact cruise lines for information about jobs available aboard cruise ships. Royal Caribbean International, Princess, Carnival, and Holland Lines have the largest fleets, but opportunities abound for short- and long-term jobs aboard smaller specialty ships.

Ben, seventy, a graduate archeologist, was widowed ten years ago. He owns a home in Indiana but rents it out half the year while he lives aboard a cruise ship and lectures on the history of ruins near Central American ports where the ship docks. Grace, in her late fifties, teaches yoga on ships that cruise between Los Angeles and Puerta Vallarta.

A sampling of life on a boat may be had in Oakland and San Francisco with Dockside Boat & Bed. This idea, launched in 1989, offers moored boats for weekends or longer. Breakfast arrives on board in a basket at the time designated. The boats are sublet by their owners through a broker—much as you would rent your home for a vacation period. A sample weekend will let you assess whether or not the close quarters of a small boat are tolerable.

For those accustomed to permanent quarters, the idea of roving from place to place—even for pay—may not appeal. Indeed, it is daunting to leave a traditional home, its basement and attic filled with family history and its garage overflowing with mementos, tools, and machinery. However, as we have explored in previous chapters, sometimes a move is necessary for health, financial, or wanderlust reasons—or simply for a change.

Checklist of Moveable Habitat Choices

Below is a summary list of the many ways to sample your moveable feast of choices as you decide whether you want to plant your roots in one place or keep roving 'til you get it right.

- Mobile home on private property

- Mobile home in a park
- Motor home
- Fifth wheel
- Travel trailer
- Live aboard a boat
- Be a seasonal snowbird
- Be a year-round snowbird
- Become a campground host
- Get a cruise ship job

5

Memorable Moves

Everyone has at least one story of a move that is memorable for its disasters or its delights. My friend Ellen held an executive position with a Maryland firm. In a happy but too-quick turn of events, she was upgraded to a new position in the company's San Francisco office. She had only three days notice and no time to pack anything but a suitcase. She contacted a nationwide van line that promised to carefully box her china, glassware, and clothing, pad her furniture and transport them to her new location in California within a week. True to their word, her neatly packaged belongings and furnishings arrived at her new quarters on schedule.

As she unloaded a carton labeled "kitchen," a distinctive essence wafted up from the box. The meticulous movers had packaged the contents of her garbage pail—double wrapped, of course—but still emitting a revolting odor.

Plan Ahead

My husband and I faced another kind of inflexible moving date. In our case, however, we were not going to a vital new executive position and our move was set months ahead.

The final week of December 1972 ended our commitments to our Southern California jobs. We were happy and excited about early retirement and our move to a small town in the San Joaquin Valley of California, 200 miles from our West Covina condominium. We had given our bosses this date three months in advance. From there, as journalists say, we "backed into" our deadline.

I was fifty, my husband fifty-eight, and we were gung-ho to launch a new life with clean air in our lungs and a clear view of the magnificent Sierra that bordered the Valley. Our basic plan—subsequently adjusted several times—was to subsist on rural acreage where we would raise farm animals and a garden.

First Mobile Home

We had been invited to begin our rural adventure on the 120-acre ranch property of dear friends. Our hosts, the Zimm family, had a lovely home but no space for our family of three: Charles, his fourteen-year-old son, youngest of our combined family of eight children, and me. Anyway we wanted independent quarters. We decided to purchase a mobile home, and the Zimms designated a space on their property where we could place it.

Planning to do all the moving by ourselves from the Southern California home, we bought a small utility trailer that could be towed by our 1970 Datsun. During the two months before finally turning over the key of our modern condominium to the young doctor who had purchased it (we saved realtor fees by selling it ourselves), we towed a trailer load of furnishings every weekend to the new property. By the time we made our last trip, the only pieces left to transport were towels from our morning showers, bedding and mattresses (we had moved the frames earlier) the coffee pot, the past week's laundry, and the garment bag of office suits worn during our final week at work.

We had chosen a new double-wide mobile home with three bedrooms and two baths, buying it from a sales lot in our new community. It was fairly simple and inexpensive to install separate meters on the Zimm property for our electricity, water, and natural gas connections. On each trip from Southern California to the mobile home, Charles and I camped out in its master bedroom using sleeping bags placed on the floor atop inflatable mattresses. While there, we took care of mutually agreed-upon tasks. He worked outside clearing weeds, mending fences, and building animal pens while I unpacked the boxes we'd brought north. I had time to install shelf paper, place items in cupboards as I unpacked them, and arrange (and rearrange!) furniture.

A lifelong goal of my industrial engineer husband was to raise pedigree pigs in his retirement. I had grown up on a farm but had scant acquaintance with the porcine element of the animal kingdom. However, I shared with him a desire for the rural life. We were not entirely surprised when Southern California friends translated the name of our new town from Porterville to "Porkerville" when they addressed our Christmas cards.

Moving a Mobile Home

The Zimm Ranch was the first location for our mobile home. We liked the life so well that after a year we decided to purchase our own mini-ranch. It was about five miles from the Zimm property. Our new acreage had a small 1940s-era cottage, badly in need of refurbishing. The cottage had its own septic tank. One water well served the whole acreage. Although there was ample space for our mobile home, the local planning department declared that the utilities for the cottage could not be extended to the mobile home. To service it, we had to plumb the mobile home for butane gas, have a septic tank installed, and a power pole set to bring electricity from the street. For water, the only extra expense was the pipe to bring water across our property from the well. Cable service was required for our TV, as our location behind a hill prevented reception of direct TV communication. These costs were outlined by the realtor who handled our purchase of the property.

The original cost of the mobile home had included delivery of the two halves of the double-wide to the property of our friends. However, when we wanted to transport it to our own property, we bore the expense of hiring professional mobile home movers to do the job. They had to unbolt the two halves, seal the openings with sheets of plastic, mount each half on a huge flatbed trailer, tow it to the new location, and set it on concrete pads prepared for it in advance. The great advantage, however, was that we needed to box only the breakables and could leave most of the furniture in place. After the two units were placed on the property, we saved a little money by reinstalling the skirting— the strips of matching metal that conceal the underpinnings of the mobile home—ourselves. Charles built us a front and back porch and we planted a garden and raised a few chickens, calves, and pigs.

With funds from his Social Security, the rent of a second property we still held in Southern California, and the meat and vegetable harvests from our mini-ranch, we managed just fine. To further supplement our income, we refurbished the little cottage on the property and rented it to grateful young tenants.

Absentee Landlord

Some better-half movers may want to hedge their bets when leaving the family homestead by retaining ownership of that property—just in case they want to return to it. My experience has included moving away from, but retaining the ownership of the properties on two different occasions—once with a husband and once on my own. Financially this was good in some—but not all—respects.

When Charles and I moved to the country, we sold our new, modern condominium, as reported above. However, we kept another, older home, and found a tenant for it without assistance from a realtor or rental agency. Retaining the older home and renting it gave us the security of knowing we had a familiar nest to return to in case our rural experiment did not work out.

While we lived in the condo we were within a few miles of that older, rented property and could personally check on the tenants every month or so. However, when we moved 200 miles away, we could no longer monitor the tenants frequently. They were an employed, unmarried man and his aged mother. We had chosen them over the young couple who wanted it, feeling that Bob and Mom were more needful and stable. They expressed their gratitude by paying the rent promptly and keeping up the lawns and flower borders. We had been absentee landlords for a year, too busy on our mini-ranch to personally visit our renters, when a neighbor we had known during the time we lived in the home let us know we should visit our tenants promptly.

Alarmed, Charles drove to the city and learned that our tenants, not wanting to bother their busy landlord, were dealing with a leaking water heater in the garage by sopping up the water with cat litter. The damage included rotted cabinets and mildewed garage walls as well as the need to replace the water heater. We concluded that absentee property management was not appropriate for us. By that time, we were convinced that life in the country was our destiny, and we sold that city home.

Moving Up

Though we loved raising and marketing pigs, it was demanding work. After four years of intensive farm life, we were tired, and the income was not that vital. We wanted to remain in the rural setting but it was time to provide a place we could host our entire brood and back away from the twenty-four-hour surveillance required for livestock.

At the time of this second "retirement," Charles was seventy and I was sixty-two. We found a Victorian, two-story, four-bedroom home which was large enough to entertain all the children and grandchildren at holiday time. We retained ownership of the mini-ranch property, finding renters for both the mobile home and cottage. We could check on these tenants regularly, as our new home was only five miles from the mini-ranch.

Our beloved Victorian had a large living room and separate dining room. We redesigned and furnished the original four sleeping rooms as a master bedroom, a guest bedroom, an office and small sitting room. Both of the latter rooms could be quickly converted to bedrooms. We added bedroom and dining room furniture, scouting yard sales for good buys.

Moving Down

After eight years at our Victorian home, once again the size of the property and its maintenance responsibilities were more than we wanted. Our children had established their own homes and were busy with careers that allowed them little free time for travel to see us and never all at the same time. We needed to downsize our property. A smaller house in town was the choice for our fourth move in "Porkerville."

A yard sale reduced the furnishings to the appropriate pieces to fulfill our needs in the smaller home. I was happy to have fewer square feet to vacuum and be in a location that put me within blocks—instead of miles—of grocery shopping. Once again, we did the moving ourselves. We moved loads to the new home daily in the same utility trailer we had purchased to move our goods from Southern California.

Moving Again

When I sold that home after my husband died and bought a two-bedroom, 1,100-square-foot cabin in the pines, another yard sale was required. This one was major and the funds realized from the two-day event more than paid for renting the seventeen-foot long U-Haul that one son and I loaded for the next move to the destination 250 miles away.

Of course, as noted earlier, the mountain home was not the final location I had expected it to be. I loved it, but to help my boomer children ease into the better halves of their own lives and lessen their concern for the latter days of mine, I then chose a Central Coast location midway between birth children in Northern California and stepchildren in the Los Angeles basin.

Pros & Cons of Property Ownership

As I planned to leave my mountain home, I remembered that city property my husband and I kept as a hedge, twenty years earlier, and now I wanted to retain ownership of my the mountain place in case the projected new life on the California Coast did not meet my expectations. However, I remembered just as clearly the earlier lesson in absentee ownership and the experience of the water heater disaster.

Mindful of the lesson Charles and I learned about personally managing a rental from great distance, I engaged a property management agent who found me a tenant who signed a year's lease. The agency investigated the fiscal responsibility of the lessee, handled the personal negotiations with her, and collected and forwarded the monthly rent to me. Under our contract, the agency saw that my property was properly kept up and the utility bills paid. The agent's 10 percent commission was money well spent. By the time the year's lease was up, I was confident I had made the right decision about my new location on the Central Coast. I put the mountain home into the hands of the real estate broker who sold it for me—eventually.

That "eventually" is a key concept and one that all mature movers should consider if they are depending on income from a leased property to at least pay the bills for that property. The agent did not find a buyer for five months. During those five months, I had no income from the property yet still had to meet the bills associated with it.

Fortunately, I was collecting monthly mortgage payments for the rural property in Porterville that was our first mini-ranch. Income from this note took care of the costs of the mountain property as I waited for its sale.

Property ownership and management can be both enjoyable and lucrative. During a part of our ranching experience, when my husband and I were in our late fifties and sixties, we purchased an apartment building of six units, and became engaged in managing tenants as well as pedigree Duroc pigs.

I have to say that in some ways tenants were more difficult than pigs. The animals didn't talk back and the only property destruction with the pigs was an occasional broken fence.

As with all property ownership, there are burdens as well as advantages. Consider how best to balance the factors of leasing your property or selling it and whether you can afford an unknown time factor between hanging out your "For Sale" sign and collecting a satisfactory price.

I treasure these experiences for what they have taught me, but my goals for my better-half-of-life are to be free of physical and financial burdens and unwanted time commitments. For me, at this point in my life, I don't want to be a landlord—absentee or otherwise.

Make Your Move Memorable
(for the Right Reasons) Checklist

- Plan well ahead if yours will be a do-it-yourself move.
- Consider retaining ownership of your previous domicile so you can "escape" back if you desire.
- If you do decide to retain ownership, ask yourself if you wish to take care of the responsibilities of being an absentee landlord, or if you should engage a property management company.
- If you are thinking of buying a mobile home (with the idea of moving the home itself if you decide to move again), look into the anticipated costs of moving it before making a final decision.

The Die Is Cast

Until the day you lock up the Big Three:

- the decision to move,
- the selection of your new location, and
- the type of housing for your new roots,

you're probably in limbo. You've revised list after list. But the moment of decision must eventually arrive and...ahhh! The peace that comes with a decision!

Truth in Moving

A compatible partner with whom you can make the big decisions—and the nagging little ones—can be a major help. But here is a caution: Based on more than sixty years of experience, including marriage, divorce, remarriage, and widowhood, and, by now, ten years of single life, and with a total of eight children involved at one time or another, I'm sharing these ironclad truths:

- The time required to make a major decision is exponentially increased by the number of people involved in making it.

- Though pets are not in on the decision-making process, moving them will add complications.
- Friends and family will volunteer the most advice *after* you have announced your final decision. Nobody really believes you have decided to move life, limb, and property until they see you bringing home empty cardboard boxes from the grocery store.

Who's in Charge?

You'll get lots of advice from people genuinely concerned for your happiness. They may take it upon themselves to investigate and remind you that there's no branch of your favorite organizations, Questing Quilters and Garden Plotters, in the new area you have chosen. In addition, relatives, especially children, will have their own ideas, not to speak of their own agendas. And, most will have strong opinions about what you should keep, sell, throw away, or give away.

An individual really has no choice but to reject all but the advice she or he wholeheartedly agrees with and take charge—whatever the consequences.

Who Owns Your Possessions?

It is well to remember the old saw, *You can't take it with you.* This is a truism we know to be right—in principle. But most of us disregard it in practice. We continue

Taking Charge of Your Moving Adventure

I'd still be sitting on a Southern California door-step, five miles from the Magic Kingdom, if I'd waited after my divorce to be touched by the wand of instant wisdom.

Up until that time, I'd had scant practice in individual decision making. Now, not only the physical chores but the decisions were mine. I had to rely on myself and pray that my choices would be reasonably good ones. Eventually, I garnered lots of hands-on training in the business of taking charge—not to speak of excellent training in recovering from mistakes.

Whether you welcome change or fear it, shucking the comfy old slippers of security to don the hiking boots of a moving adventure requires lots of decisions, possibly more than you have ever made before and probably more than you really ever wanted to make. If this is the case, don't worry; you'll be surprised how resourceful you can be when you need to be!

to haul possessions around with us as though taking leave of any of our precious stuff is equivalent to abandoning a child. Do we really own our possessions, or do they own us?

I grew up on a small dairy farm with mail-order-motley furnishings. Durable couches and chairs were covered with washable throws so that dusty overalls would not soil the print cushions. The floor surfaces were linoleum—the easier to clear of muddy boot tracks. Any member of the Association of Interior Decorators would have recommended burning the furnishings, probably the whole house. Perhaps, this history is why, for me, a chair is a chair is a chair.

Yes, I treasure things I've saved for years: a potholder handwoven by one son in kindergarten, juvenile drawings that reveal early talents eventually realized, letters exchanged with my sister documenting our lives when our children were growing up. I've kept a few watercolors painted by a talented friend—and many photos. These are precious to me, and they—not antique tables, credenzas, or *objets d'art*—are the heart of my home. I enjoy fine art pieces and furnishings in museums and in other people's homes, but I am always grateful to admire them without being responsible for them.

Practical essentials surround me: a utilitarian desk and computer, a bed, a bookcase, a chest for clothing, and large file cabinets. The latter must be weeded periodically, because I'm an addicted paper saver—articles, news clippings, family history records, photos, and countless written memos.

I'm not advocating the reduction of furnishings to a straight-back chair, a TV, and a pallet on the floor. Adequate furniture and appliances are required if we are to live in reasonable comfort. However for most of my friends and acquaintances, "reasonable comfort" includes expensive furnishings, beautiful antiques and valuable collections. And, these are housed within homes that are as precious as their contents—and as equally unlikely to be left behind for new horizons.

Collectors of Note

My friend Doris, a former librarian, readily admits that her possessions have a hold on her. The modest home she occupies could easily earn entrance fees as an art gallery.

The living room, dining room, and each bedroom has at least one wall of books. All other walls are covered with framed and unframed original drawings, paintings, collages, prints, tapestries, and fabric art. The book inventory runs close to two thousand titles—and is growing. Doris rarely rereads them or, by her admission, even dusts them.

Can she take all the books and art with her? No. But she loves every piece. They are part of who she is and the thought of parting with even one of her collection pains her. She will probably donate the lot—eventually—to an art museum and library. "I've certainly moved it all for the last time," she says. Recently turned sixty, she keeps busy in her "better years" with children, grandchildren, assisting in a flower shop, and writing her memoirs.

Another friend, Mark, seventy-two, is moving inland from the coast to Colorado. A former teacher and world traveler, his hobbies have included rock climbing, skiing, camping—activities he can no longer pursue. A daily walk is the limit of his physical abilities now.

However, stashed in the twenty-four-foot motor home he has purchased for his exodus from California are pitons, ropes, tents, and sleeping bags used for climbs in the Sierra and the Himalayas; five pairs of skis; snowshoes; Coleman lanterns and stoves; ski and hiking boots.

Mark is a linguist, a talented writer, and charming conversationalist. Intelligent as he is, he seems not to realize that the only "things" he really needs are his capacity to explore ideas and share through conversation or writing the wealth of experiences that have made his life exciting.

His accumulation reminds me of Mildred and Arthur, friends from long ago. Then in his late seventies, Arthur, a gardener with the Jolly Green Giant touch, planted string beans, limas, and corn each year of the ten years I knew them.

All products would have commanded premium prices at the local farmers' market. But Arthur did not sell them. Instead, these crops were harvested and preserved—by Mildred, of course—in Mason jars. If both had lived to be 200, they could not have consumed all the canned goods— some of which Mildred secretly dispensed to her friends. They built an extra room onto the garage to accommodate the shelves of jarred produce. I'm sure that, in Arthur's mind, if they had enough "laid by" they would survive to consume it all.

If your household is a gallery like Doris' or a storage facility like Mark's or Arthur's and if moving time has arrived, leaving behind or even transporting the precious objects is far more threatening than moving a household like mine. Nothing is impossible, however, so bear with me as we explore the possibilities.

What Fits Your New Life?

The decision to move has been made. But not all your beloved possessions will fit into the new quarters. At first you believe you cannot part with a single piece. The Queen Anne chair has been in the family for generations. The Hummel figures collection and your father's leather-bound classics are too precious to let go.

Your cedar chest holds your wedding dress (or dresses) and other mementos of such sentimental worth that you feel like canceling all moves—forever. Although you've treasured these possessions for years, you are starting a new life. One of its names is "freedom," and you must lighten both the physical and emotional loads you carry.

By the time you become a superadult, chances are that no more than two people are voting. Even the most compatible couples may disagree about what to fit into the new quarters. For example, the exercise tapes of Denise Austin or Jane Fonda will be easier to pack, transport, and store than a Stairmaster or exercise bike. If you are a moving pair, be sure to make separate *his* and *her* lists so that you can weigh the storage needs before final priorities are set on what to take with you.

Paring Down Possessions

Collecting furniture, tools, and implements of all kinds appears to be an addiction in our modern United States culture. One need only browse the newspapers' classified sections to be aware of the proliferation of garage sales and yard sales. I call them Stuff Sales (see Chapter 9).

In every community I've called home, "stuff" flows from household to household. People regularly get rid of old or used furniture and tools so they can upgrade. In many cases, they are about to move and find that no van is large enough to carry it all.

For some, the weekend treasure tour of yard and garage sales is a form of recreation. A columnist recently wrote that she commandeers her husband's truck on Saturdays so that she can more easily haul the finds she discovers. She marks a map of her town on Friday evening and sets out at dawn on Saturday. "You have to get there early or all the good stuff will be gone," she warns.

When my husband and I moved from a Victorian, two-story, four-bedroom home, with outbuildings that housed animals and the machinery we needed to maintain five acres, we were fortunate to be able to sell the riding lawn mower and the orchard and animal-tending tools to the purchaser of the property.

Our beloved farmhouse had a large living room and separate dining room. Its four sleeping rooms were variously furnished as a master bedroom, a guest bedroom, an office, and a small "sitting room" that could be quickly converted to another bedroom when the children visited. A yard sale reduced the pieces of furniture to those needed to furnish the three-bedroom, 1,800-square-foot house we moved to next.

When I sold that home after my husband died and purchased a two-bedroom home of 1,100 square feet, another yard sale was required. It more than paid for that move.

In my long and mobile history, I have had much to enjoy wherever I relocated. I treasured new groups of friends in each new location. Communities I've lived in include Washington DC, small towns in Alabama, and Atlanta, Georgia. I was fascinated with rearing our children and the various responsibilities of mother, stepmother, and journalist. Each location and job—volunteer or paid—filled a current need and enthusiasm, but few pieces of furniture or other possessions have had enough importance to be carried wherever I went.

Transferring Pets

For many of us, a pet is as treasured as a human friend. Among my friends is a senior lady who wants to sell her four-bedroom home—where she lives alone—and move to the more sociable atmosphere of a retirement facility. However, she will not disrupt the comfort of her beloved poodle, now very old and nearly blind. Only "when Toby goes" will she consider moving.

Moving an animal to new quarters can be frustrating for both animal and owner. If you are driving your own vehicle to a new location, your pet will be one of the valuables, along with your camera and laptop, that you carry in your car or for which you make special transfer arrangements.

If your cat or dog does not have an identifying collar or some kind of electronic locating device, one of your earliest responsibilities once you have chosen your destination is to get identification tags or collars that bear your new address and telephone number.

Dogs are reputed to identify location more by odor than sight. You have a scent that helps the canine identify you as its master. But the dog may panic in a strange place and break out in its effort to find you. If it gets lost during the inevitable confusion during a move, his collar tag, inscribed with your new location and telephone number, may be your only chance of retrieving him. Keep a clear, up-to-date photo of your pet. This will be a great help in the event it is lost during or after a move.

Cats are more territorial and can be acclimated after arrival if kept in a confined area such as a bathroom for two or three days with, of course, food, water, and a litterbox. As long as you feed and console kitty during this brief period of incarceration, it will be grateful to have the run of the house when released and should adapt quickly.

Birds must be protected from overheating—whether carried in your car or sent by public transport. A small water bottle of the kind provided for hamsters or gerbils may be fixed inside the cage.

One U-Haul move for me is memorable because of my uncompromising need to move my "pets"—not the four-legged or winged variety. I love houseplants and flowers. I couldn't take my garden with me, but my spider plant, philodendrons, and fuchsias, progeny of those propagated in the garden room of our farm house years earlier, had to go with me.

My son loaded them last in the big van, each in its own carton, and did everything he could to protect them. I felt I must water my babies before we left. Not good. The soaked cartons fell apart and allowed pots to smash each other during stops and starts of the heavy vehicle. For later moves I boxed the plants—unwatered—in the trunk of my car.

Real Needs

Among the utilitarian possessions that seem absolutely necessary, an automobile may top the list. However, you may want to consider selling it in favor of using public transportation. Local buses or subsidized senior transportation may mean you do not really need a car.

Artifacts of family history are to be treasured and saved. List heirlooms and irreplaceable pieces. Which will you have space for at the new location? Unless you are a key figure in the *Antiques Roadshow* or own an antiques business, storing furniture, paintings, and photographs that have no *personal* connection will only add to your burden when they have to be moved. If you feel you cannot part with these now, check the cost of public storage and consider storing them until you know what you want to do with them. Also consider transferring some family treasures to the homes of children or other relatives. (See Chapter 8.)

What is the square-footage of the new quarters compared to your present home? You will want to take your favorite lounge chair, your bed with the perfect mattress, a special reading lamp, and its end table. However, do not neglect to make sure they will fit into the new place, or you may well find yourself in a quandary when you begin to unload.

What kinds of appliances and furniture are furnished at your new location? If you are moving to a senior residence facility, most meals are included with your rental agreement and you will not need much in the line of cooking utensils. However, as happened to me, I needed a few again when I moved to an apartment. A few basics for the kitchen may be worth keeping as insurance.

You may still be uneasy about having "cast the die" to embrace a new venue for your best years. But when you must move for health, financial, family-proximity reasons, or as a result of a natural disaster, accept the inevitable, and unload your accumulated, but unnecessary "stuff" and welcome the search for new opportunities.

Even if we have not suffered losses through fire, flood, tornado, or earthquake, the news media keep us aware of people who lose everything in such catastrophes.

What do they have left but their lives and their unique

selves? These are the most important requirements for a fresh start anywhere.

Decisions Checklist

- Listen to good advice but rely on your own judgment.
- Ask yourself if you own your possessions or if they own you.
- Consider examples of chronic "stuff keepers." Do they resemble you?
- Be realistic about what will fit the dimensions of your new life.
- Do you really need to keep an automobile?
- If you decide to keep it, does it require a garage and is one available at the new place?
- Consider storing or giving family heirlooms to children or other relatives.

7

Taming the Moving Tiger

By now you have conquered most of the moving tremors or at least subdued them enough to begin the steps that will get you and your possessions moved to the new location. You resolve to start today, but just thinking about the plethora of tasks ahead makes you want to melt into the cushions of your easy chair. A gazillion things to do *first* buzz about in your head like flies at a barbecue.

Where to Start?

There are many ways to get ready for a move and you will think of short cuts on your own as you work through the process. Here are some of my suggestions for what needs to be done first.

First of all, get organized! Organization will give you a sense of confidence, a sense of purpose, and, most important, a sense of commitment to your move. Allow at least a month for planning and preparation.

Purchase—if you do not have them already—a spiral notebook and a calendar with boxes large enough for notations. These will help with your countdown and enable you to visualize the number of tasks and the number of days before your departure date. (I like the decisive black of ink and don't mind the cross-outs, but one fellow mover, Rose, cannot abide an untidy page so she makes her lists in pencil and wears out a dozen erasers in the process. Suit yourself. Pencil or ink won't be important to the final move.)

Label the notebook cover simply "Move," or something more imaginative like "Liberty Launch" or "Destination Delight"—whatever strikes your fancy. This book will contain your master list, the minor lists, and serve to record inevitable changes.

The first entry on page one should be the address of your new location along with pertinent names and telephone numbers. For instance, if you are moving to a senior residential facility, record the name and phone number of the manager or anyone there you may need to contact. If you are dealing with a real estate agent—either listing the home you are leaving or to purchase or rent a new home—his or her name, address, and phone number go on this page.

File Folders

In a convenient central location install a portable box—one wide and deep enough to hold file folders—or clear out a drawer of equal capacity. The kitchen drawer that had held my supply of hand towels (more than I ever used) was my choice during one move.

This box or drawer will be used exclusively as your file of move information. Be sure each folder is labeled. And, stock enough folders so that you can add new titles as subject matter demands. Arrange them alphabetically—unless you have a better system.

One file folder will hold loose memos, receipts, bills, miscellaneous business cards and flyers. Another will hold important business papers such as the agreement listing costs, amenities, and house rules at your new site.

One folder will hold such essentials as a rough-sketch floor plan including the square footage of your new house, cottage, apartment, or room. (You took measurements of the layout including window and door locations, didn't you?) Include a list of the furnishings, if any, provided at your new location.

The destination folder (the one labeled with the name of your new community) holds brochures about cable TV hookup, flyers featuring church locations, and booklets from the chamber of commerce, Welcome Wagon, and community hostesses.

You may also want a folder for helpful hints you are saving from Heloise or other sources. One folder will hold information about moving van companies, do-it-yourself truck rentals such as U-Haul, and storage lockers. You will throw most of this away eventually but for now, just organizing these folders will give you a good feeling. Already you have accomplished a number of important tasks before you begin to pack anything.

The Time Line

Timing is everything, we are told. I agree—providing you can be flexible. I disagree, however, if you make timing a god to worship. If you are somewhat overwhelmed by this whole chore, as most of us are, flexibility as to timing will lessen frustration, get the jobs done more easily, and bring you through the moving process more or less on schedule. Still, some dates are rigid, such as the day and time the moving company—if you use one—is to show up at your front door.

Allow extra time for all arrangements that are outside your individual control.

Following are suggestions for the timing of certain elements common to most moves. They cover mainly the tasks involved if you do all or most of your own packing. Even if a moving company is transporting all your worldly goods, you still have basic chores—packing or disposing of essential belongings and personal items. Tip: Commercial moving companies will not insure the safety of your goods unless their employees do the packing.

Deadline Dates

Circle in red on your calendar the first date you can take occupancy at the new location. Although you can probably arrive later than the take-occupancy date, sooner is normally not possible and later usually adds to your expenses at the current location. If you own your current property and plan to rent or lease it, circle in red also, the date of promised occupancy for the new tenant. Keep at least a week's time between your scheduled departure and the day the new tenant moves in, both as a buffer in case your schedule gets delayed and to give you time to clean or to have the property cleaned for your tenant.

Post Office Guides

The United States Postal Service packet entitled *Mover's Guide* offers moving tips and includes money-saving coupons for items and services people who are moving often have need of, such as storage facilities and return address labels.

As soon as you know your date of arrival at the new location fill out the post card form that tells the post office where to forward your mail. Turn this in personally at the post office even though the information may be sent without charge on the postcard provided. We are warned that postcards that list address changes can sometimes get into the wrong hands. Clever thieves and burglars know that there are periods between move-out and move-in when doors are unlocked. Precious goods are sometimes stacked outside a home and temporarily left unguarded.

In the post office *Mover's Guide* are a few change-of-address notification cards you can use to send to subscription services and other regular correspondents. You probably have more than three correspondents, so pick up several kits. They are free. As with the post office change of address form, do not mail them as postcards. Put them in envelopes to mail to your correspondents.

Don't forget to go through your personal address book sending cards to each person listed so you don't stand the chance of losing contact with friends and relatives. You are welcome to borrow the little ditty that was the inspiration for the name of this book (see the "Introduction" at the front of this book).

To change your subscription address for magazines, check the opening pages of current issues. At the bottom of the column that lists the editorial staff is information for change of address. Do not send your address change to the editorial address. This delays action. Even if you notify a periodical's subscription services department two months in advance, it often takes longer to get the service switched.

The post office will forward first-class mail and most subscriptions for a year. Your monthly credit card and utility statements always come with a form on which you can provide address changes.

"The greatest pitfall for me," says a fellow frequent mover, "is getting addresses changed. It's such an ongoing task. I keep a list of each entity or person I have informed of my new address and the date I gave the information so as not to waste time in renotifying the same people and same magazines."

It is a good idea also to create a pleasant rapport with whoever is moving into the place you leave, because inevitably there are slipups in mail forwarding. Filling out address change notifications is a good job for the end of the day when you're too tired to lift anything heavier than a pencil.

Telephone Service

Call your telephone service operator. The appropriate number is on your monthly statement as well as in the phone directory. Once you connect with the service operator (this may require waiting through several rock and roll or bluegrass arias), tell him that you want service connected at your new address by the date you have set for your move-in. He'll also need to know the cutoff date at your present phone. If your move will be completed in one day, you may ask for the cutoff to be the same day as the new connect.

If your move requires several trips back and forth, keep your telephone service at the old address until you lock the door for the last time.

Always request the telephone company's new-number notification service (the "number has been changed to…" message), which is usually offered without extra charge for at least a month after you cancel the old phone.

When your service is simply a transfer within the same company, ask first that you be able to keep your old number. If this isn't possible, ask what your new number will be. Normally, the service operator can give it to you at that time. He will suggest you not have it printed on business cards or stationery until you receive final confirmation of the number.

If your new phone is to be served by a different company, you can usually get that company's 800 number from the company you are leaving and make your new arrangements by phone. (Keep your memo book handy so you can accurately give your destination address. New information has a way of vanishing from our minds when we least expect.)

There is a charge for switching your telephone service, though most companies will allow you to pay on a three-month basis, without carrying charges.

Speaking of telephones, keep in your possession a telephone book from the community you are leaving. After you settle in at the new location, you may wish to contact businesses, services, and friends whose numbers and addresses are not in your personal address book.

Essential Utilities

Call your gas and electric company. If you are leasing or renting your old residence and the new tenant is moving in promptly, ask to have the utilities kept on and have the final bill sent to your new address. Ask that your new tenant promptly switch service to his or her name. If the lease is being handled by a real estate agency, its representative will advise the new lessee to sign up for these services.

Get It in Writing

When you personally handle the lease or rental of the property you are leaving, get a signed contract. This agreement will detail what the tenant is responsible for in the way of utilities and property upkeep. Even if your lessee is a beloved daughter, your favorite nephew, or your twin brother, get your agreement in writing on a form you can devise yourself or on an official rent or lease form, available at stationery stores. Get signatures. Whatever the personal relationship with your new tenant, this is a business arrangement. It is a protection for your tenant as well as for yourself when all parties know the rules of engagement. Neither wants to wind up dealing with the rules of war.

Bank & Safe Deposit Box

If your bank of record has a branch in your new community, you need only inform your bank of your change of address. Most banks will be happy to service your account during your move. If you wish to place your account with a new bank, do so after you become better acquainted with the new community.

The bank at my mountain community did not have a branch at my new location. Before I switched banks, I explored my new area and found one that was within walking distance from my retirement home destination. I rented a safe deposit box and transferred important documents to it before my final move rather than risk misplacing them in the confusion of the move.

Since I have my Social Security check automatically deposited, this was a matter that could be handled with a request over my signature at the new bank.

The Catch-All Corners

Choose a corner of each room of your current location where you can begin stacking boxes for your move. Even though you may consider this an unsightly scar on your otherwise perfectly kept home, you are about to test your housekeeping skills in an entirely new way, and intention now is to create as much ease in the moving process as possible. Remove all furniture and occasional rugs from this corner. Remove paintings or other wall hangings that will be difficult to reach when the boxes begin to stack up. This corner's stack of boxes should not hamper access for moving large pieces of furniture that your mover may decide to load before these boxes.

Vital Tools

Before you begin to pack anything, four essentials must be in hand:

- Tape. Buy a roll or two of pressure-sensitive sealing tape that can be used to seal the boxes you pack or to reconstruct ones that are flattened.
- Marking pen. Buy a bright colored marking pen that you will use to *label* every single box—on top and on at least one side or end. (Labels on the tops of boxes are unreadable when the boxes are stacked.) The importance of labeling every box cannot be overstated. Resist the temptation to label any box, "Miscellaneous."

  One mover suggests that, to simplify labeling and avoid having to list contents of a box on its lid, you may want to create a control list in your notebook, where writing is easier than the lean-and-stretch associated with labeling boxes. Instead of listing every item in the box, label it "Kitchen 1," "Kitchen 2," etc. Your note book control list will show the items in that box.

  You may be so grateful for having followed this advice to label boxes that you will want to create a cross-stitch sampler for your progeny: "Label Now Or Lament Later." But save doing this happy chore until after you move.
- Newspaper. Most of today's newspapers are printed with ink that does not rub off easily. The daily news can be used to wrap and pad dishes, kitchenware, and fragile items.

  Bubble wrap and plastic peanuts are excellent but must be purchased and are more difficult to corral and discard later. The moment you know you are going to move, start saving the daily papers and the throwaways from your driveway.

• Large plastic bags. Though wardrobe boxes are available from moving companies, large plastic trash bags are less expensive and will efficiently carry and protect most towels, clothing and bedding. Just make sure no one gets confused and throws out half of your wardrobe!

Best Boxes in Town

You can purchase sturdy boxes of all sizes from retailers like Mail Boxes Etc., Office Depot, or from the nearest moving company. Spend your money as you wish, but you do not have to buy cardboard boxes. With all my moves, I have yet to purchase one.

My target for perfect boxes is the neighborhood liquor store. Beer and spirits of all brands arrive daily in sturdy boxes exactly the right size for the do-it-yourself mover.

For my latest move, I alerted the store owner to my needs and learned that every midafternoon, they flatten cardboard boxes for recycling. They were happy to save whole ones for me if I collected them no later than 3 P.M. on a given day. I was able to fit at least a dozen per trip into the trunk and back seat of my little sedan.

Because my most recent move was only twelve miles and I had the option of storing books and office materials at my new address before my living quarters were available, I made frequent trips in my car using and reusing my boxes.

One friend who formerly sold Avon products suggests that you contact the local Avon lady for boxes. Their products are shipped in plastic-lined containers, and normally these salesladies have more boxes than space to store them.

What to Pack First

Begin with the books you cannot live without. Books are heavy and it is our good fortune that many of the liquor store boxes have grip slots in two ends—ideal handles for lifting boxes of books.

As you consider your shelves of books, check your sketch and dimensions of the space you are to occupy. How many bookshelves and how many books will the new space hold? Which ones may be welcomed as donations to your local library? All those you don't need until you arrive at the new location can be packed now. Boxed books can be stacked deeply without damage and they make an ideal foundation for lighter items.

You may be tempted to first pack the small objects from your whatnot shelves—the pieces you enjoy looking at each day but do not touch—unless you are compulsive about dusting. Do not pack any of these until you know you will have space for them in the new location. Those you plan to put in storage, sell, or give away should remain on your shelves for later attention.

Room Survey

With your notebook in hand, go to each room. Label the top of a page with the name of the room. List the items *you do not use daily* but want to take with you. Obviously, these are the things to pack at once. In the kitchen, for instance, how many pots, pans, bowls, and utensils do you use daily? How much glassware and how many place settings of dishes? Don't stint, but be practical. Some of these items may be ones you want to offer at your "loot party" (see Chapter 8).

Survey the bathroom toiletry drawers and medicine cabinets and the caverns under sinks. How often do you use the bottles, jars, cleaning fluids, brushes and cloths? Dispose of everything that isn't essential to your health and comfort. Be sure to retain in the bathroom and kitchen the implements and products you will need to do a final cleaning, whether you hire it done or do it yourself. Also, keep a full roll of toilet paper on its spindle!

If you are more comfortable "talking" your list than writing it, you may wish to record the room information on tape. Some of our best ideas come as we are driving or waiting in traffic lines. Taping messages while in the car is another way of making sure your best moving ideas are captured until they can be implemented.

Sigh of Relief Checklist

Double check to make sure you have:

- marked your calendar
- assembled your file folders
- begun your notebook lists
- made your reservations for a van line or rental equipment
- gathered sealing tape, marking pen, plastic bags, and boxes

- visited the post office for copies of the *Mover's Guide*
- called your phone and utility companies
- made notations about room-by-room packing sequence
- arranged for future tenants, property manager or sale.

Voila! You have at least cornered, if not tamed, the "moving tiger." Your move plan is organized.

Keep your notebook handy. You are now set to plan for dealing with "stuff overload." We tackle that job in the next chapter.

B

Dealing with "Stuff Overload"

I don't want to offend anyone by calling precious collections and other valuable possessions "stuff." But as we prepare for a move, sorting and packing, even the most astute judges of fine art may begin to describe it all as "stuff." Don't despair. Often much of the accumulated furniture, linens, figurines, glassware and tableware can be safely housed beneath the roofs of friends or family members or stored in a commercial facility.

Needs vs. Wants

The size of your new quarters and the amount of storage space available in it are the major factors in determining what you can move and what you have to store, give away, or sell. For example, if you are going to a retirement complex that provides all or most of your meals, you do not need the slow cooker, the bread maker or the set of Mikasa china. A new friend at The Palms shared with me the fact that on unpacking she found—to her embarrassment—a box of jelly glasses. "It took me a while to get out of the habit of storing things I thought I might use in the future."

As reported earlier, during my first visit to The Palms I recorded the dimensions of the apartment I'd chosen and sketched the location of doorways and windows. This gave me a picture of what I could use—whether my favorite bookcase would fit under the window and whether there'd be room for the large watercolors I wanted to hang on the walls. I realized that no matter how much I loved my household treasures, some had to be disposed of.

The apartment was carpeted in sturdy match-everything-beige Berber. It had a bedroom and a living room connected by a bathroom. I had space for my double bed, bedside tables and lamps; my computer desk, file cabinet, a couch, a couple of occasional chairs, and a small entertainment center. A large closet had two shelves above the hanging area. The bathroom was furnished with a medicine cabinet, cupboard, drawers, and shelves under the sink.

The mountain retreat I was leaving was more than double that size and was crowded with furnishings. It had two bedrooms, one and a half baths, an office, and an open-plan living-dining room-kitchen flanked by a walk-in pantry. Wide walls held framed art as well as family pictures, and ample shelf space displayed favorite vases, plants, and bric-a-brac, including figurines and art pieces that I had received as gifts over many years. They were pleasant reminders of dear friends and relatives.

A Plethora of Pots

Over the years, the number of people I prepared meals for had graduated from first husband and three children to second husband and five stepchildren. It was fun to create new menus as well as hear acclaim when I repeated favorites.

At one time we belonged to a group called Cooks Tours in which we visited—gastronomically—a different country once a month with the responsibilities for food categories relegated to the seven member couples. Later, during my stint as a farm wife, I prepared meals daily for my husband and son and for countless visitors.

This resulted in the accumulation of enough pots, casseroles, and roasting and baking pans to furnish the kitchen of a small restaurant. By the time I reached the independence of being a single senior, I was ready to give up my role as Queen of the Range.

I looked forward to living at The Palms, where grocery shopping, menus, and food preparation were the responsibility of the kitchen staff. Therefore, my many pots, dishes, spice racks, and recipe books were no longer needed. Those Better-Half-Movers who go to individual rentals or purchase new homes with ample cupboards may want to retain most of their cooking tools, but all should take an inventory and separate what is essential from what is sentimental.

Most retirement complexes I've surveyed include meals in their monthly fees. At The Palms all residents paid for two meals per day and snacks, regardless of apartment size or whether they had a kitchen. Lunch was optional in the restaurant-like dining room at minimal cost. To serve my anticipated needs, I packed my coffeemaker, four mugs for tea or coffee, a few small plates that could be used for hors d'oeuvres, a decanter and matching glasses that were a treasured gift, and four tumblers that could be used for other drinks.

Can We Really Take It with Us?

Realistically, we know we can't take our precious possessions with us into the Great Beyond. To me, it is better to pass these valuables on to younger relatives or friends who will cherish them. To accomplish this, I invited my children to my mountaintop for a giant giveaway.

Mom's Loot Party

When I announced that I was moving from my beloved mountain home, the kids were at first shocked and made call after call to learn if I were obliquely announcing a terminal illness. They were even more concerned when I invited them to come pick out the household items they could use. Finally, assured that I was still in good health and had my wits about me, my lighthearted and ever-supportive offspring named the plan for distribution of goods "Mom's Loot Party." You may want to give your distribution plan a more genteel name, such as the "Salvation Soiree" or "Deliverance Day." Whatever you call it, the gratitude of the recipients and the reduction of things to pack should brighten your spirits, not to speak of easing the strain on your back muscles.

The children were grateful for whatever I offered and pleased to use the haul-away date as another reason for a last visit to the mountain retreat they all enjoyed. It made me happy to give away treasures and many practical items that—though worn—were welcomed. The kids made me promise to visit my donated possessions at their homes often.

Actually, distributing the loot turned into a series of informal gatherings. These were held on any day the recipients could come to the mountain. Busy as they were, most chose different days and this was good in several ways. With the house in disarray and boxes—both empty and packed—piling up, it was simpler to host no more than two children at a time. But I set a deadline. If they couldn't arrive within my designated nine-day time frame (two weekends and the days between), they were out of luck. The loot would go into my next major event, The Stuff Sale.

To feed these visitors, I usually ordered pizza and provided paper plates so that cookware and serving plates they planned to carry away would not be needed for our shared meals.

My mother's china had already been promised and transferred to my youngest birth son. The flatware went to my eldest son, whose initials matched those engraved on the sterling. The silver serving dishes went to the middle birth son. These things were of more sentimental value to those three than to the stepkids.

One daughter needed kitchenware. Her sister had dibs on a couple of chairs and lamp tables—but she could not take them at that time. This was fortunate for me because I had space for and needed these items in my Palms apartment. They were marked with her name and remained in my possession until my last move. This daughter loves to cook. So on her day at the loot party, she commandeered my cookbooks, some dating from the late 1940s.

One son and his wife needed towels and bed linen. Another, who had lost wall hangings and art to a faulty interior sprinkler system, was happy to have the custom-made clock that his father and I had chosen for our large farmhouse years before. It was too massive for any wall in my new quarters. The youngest stepson—who also loves to cook but changes his residence about as often as I do—cleared my shelves of spices, seasonings, and flavorings.

Family History Treasures

Before this—through the years—and because photographs are among the most valued family heirlooms, we had assembled into scrapbooks photographs and school mementos for each child. This began as our "Twenty-One Book" project. When the kids reached that age, we presented them with photo and memento records of their pasts.

Doing this was not entirely altruistic. Charles and I knew, early on, that we would not—for ourselves—take the time to organize all the accumulated photos into albums. Much better to sort and direct them to the child for whom they would be most meaningful. As all will know, assembling old photos, report cards, and news clips from the family files is extremely time-consuming.

An international organization, Creative Memories, is an excellent guide for such endeavors. For a reasonable fee, you may attend workshops led by artistic supervisors who provide appropriate pens, acid-free paper, and photo mounting aides and help guide the novice through the process of producing beautiful books that are heirlooms in themselves.

If you haven't already assembled photos for such distribution you may want to consider doing this before your next move. It takes time but is worth the effort. Any reduction in loaded boxes is a plus.

Public (or Private) Storage

In spite of my words and other warnings against harboring stuff, you may have precious items you cannot part with. Rental spaces in guarded, insured storage blocks are available in virtually every community. Investigate storage facilities and costs when you are deciding on your location.

Those who plan to store it all and take to their wheels as seasonal or year-round snowbirds will require large storage units. Find storage facilities under Mini-Storage or Self-Storage in the Yellow Pages. Such facilities are perfect for retirees who have not yet decided whether they will move back to an old home or permanently establish in a new location. Used furnishings can be stored and retrieved at less expense than purchasing new. In choosing a storage unit, consider whether it is best to rent one in your destination community or in your current community, preferably near a relative who can check on your possessions from time to time.

Betty admirably reduced her stuff, after her husband died, to what would fit into her RV. She transferred a number of furnishings from the family home to the households of a son and a daughter. However, she wanted to retain a precious dining room table and chairs and several boxes of kitchenware for possible future use. She stored them at a mini-storage facility. "Finally, I realized I was never going to use those pieces again and their storage was costing me too much. I sold the dining set and, for the kitchen stuff, I bought a small metal storage unit that fits beside my RV in the park. It is easily accessible, expands my space and, in the long run, has cost me far less than I was paying for public storage."

Marvin and Loraine moved to Hawaii to take advantage of an opportunity to "sit" a home in Maui for the first year of their retirement. They sold their Albuquerque home and put all their furnishings into storage, reserving final decision about a permanent retirement location until their return from the islands.

They had been enjoying their life in Hawaii for three months when they received a call from their storage company. The entire facility had burned to the ground and they had lost all their furnishings. Fortunately it was fully insured. "We had nothing of the old familiar things," Loraine says. "We were like newlyweds starting over when we returned to begin the next phase of our retirement."

When I left the mountains for the coast I, too, had a precious-goods storage problem. One friend near my destination was happy to have use of my mahogany cabinet and sofa, as she was beginning to furnish a new home.

Our plan was that should The Palms not work for me or if I decided to rent larger quarters, I could retrieve these pieces. Meanwhile, they were in use and being cared for. In this way, I retained furniture I loved and did not have to pay for its storage. As it turned out, I did not miss these pieces as much as I thought I would and did not have space for them again. When my friend purchased her own new furnishings, we held a yard sale on her property, and

I sold them—as well as additional odds and ends I'd accumulated in the two-year interim.

Sequence

It is now time to check your date calendar and the lists in your memo book once again. If you plan to create photo and memory albums for the children or grandchildren, be sure that you schedule this effort *before* your Loot Party and allow several days for the project—for two reasons. First, you can deliver the albums as the children visit. Mailing them later will mean high postage cost. Second, you will still have a dining table or card table to work on before these items are distributed to the "looters." A large flat surface is essential for sorting mementos, and, for most of us over fifty, a table has an advantage over the floor as a surface for assembling materials and packing boxes.

Your yard, garage, or stuff sale is the last major event before you move. Tips on how to make this sale both energy friendly and financially rewarding are presented in the next chapter.

Too Much Stuff Checklist

- Evaluate your real needs based on the size of new quarters.
- Recognize that you can't take it all with you.
- Consider giving favorite pieces to children.
- Compile family history treasures before you move.
- If renting storage space, decide whether it should

be near your destination or near your current residence.

- Consider storing favorite pieces with a friend.

The Stuff Sale

You will gain financial rewards, a sense of freedom, and have less to pack if you sell your excess stuff. As you do the countdown before your move, decide what to keep, what to store, what to give to friends and relatives, and what to sell.

Both before and since my move from the mountain, I have participated in a number of stuff sales. Here are tips for earning Trader-of-The-Day status on your block.

Remember Your Purpose

As you make your overall plan for stuff-relief, keep foremost in mind the reason you are selling items. It is not to make a financial killing; it is to dispose of goods you no longer need.

Be open to negotiation. The customer wants an item and, obviously, he should pay, but don't be mulish about requiring the price you have listed lest birds in the hand fly off to never return. Now, having said that, don't be afraid to turn down an offer that is unreasonable; someone else is likely come along—or the original guy may up his offer.

Weather Matters

Though you cannot control the weather, it is a good idea to check the average amount of rainfall or snowfall at the time you plan your sale. If the forecast is unpredictable but your move has an approaching deadline, use the interior of your garage or that of a friend to display your items. Don't forget, though, that if you use premises other than your own, you will have a time-consuming mini-move getting your gear to the sale location.

I staged one sale in my two-car garage. Rain wasn't expected, but the temperature was in the 90s. Included in my ad for the day was "Free Lemonade." For another sale, I joined with two friends to use the garage of one, as well as her wide driveway. My large pieces for sale were ones she had been storing for me. It was relatively easy to take my small stuff to her home in boxes.

Communities differ in their enthusiasm for garage and yard sales. A sale advertised as a "Moving Sale" may bring more potential buyers who know that if you are moving you will be desperate to sell and they may find better bargains. A sale advertised as a "Three Family Yard Sale" or a "Five-Family Cul-de-sac Sale" may bring larger numbers of customers who anticipate variety and quantity.

Advertising

Whatever you call your sale you may purchase space in your local newspaper to promote it. The classified section of any newspaper will show rates, usually charged by the day on a per-word or per-line basis. Check the accuracy of the ad the first day it is published. Do not include your phone number in your ad unless you welcome questions about specific items, twenty-four hours a day. Searchers will try to save time by calling ahead to learn if your sale includes a hair dryer, a Flexible Flyer, or a lawn mower, etc.

Purchasing an ad is not always necessary. Many successful sales are advertised only by hand-lettered signs posted in the immediate neighborhood a day or two before the event.

Utility companies frown on signs posted on telephone and electric power poles. Lest yours be stripped off these handy display points, use wooden stakes or wire frames that can be stabbed into the earth.

Grocery store and other public bulletin boards are usually available for placing 3 x 5 cards detailing your sale. No charge is made for this. Be sure that the information includes the date(s) and the hours your sale will be held, as well as the address where it will take place.

Clearly stating the starting hour is vital. Those who regularly attend such sales will be knocking on your door at 6 A.M. if you fail to specify the starting time. One wry entrepreneur posted a sign on her door: "All items are double price before 8 A.M."

Setting Up

More of your items will sell if you put some thought into their display. Allow enough time to organize the pieces so they are easily accessible, with pathways between display tables or benches. Arrange like items together, but do not heap them into piles that make individual articles difficult to see.

Consider Consignment

In the San Bernardino Mountains of California, in the small community of Crestline, massive yard sales are held on the weekends of Memorial Day and Labor Day.

Residents display their disposable items on front porches, decks, lawns, and driveways. They clear their vehicles from garages to create space for clothes racks, tables, and benches on which to exhibit their goods. The result is a smorgasbord of items and a bazaar-like atmosphere for those who wander or drive the streets of the community.

All vendors may participate without having to advertise, but many (for about $25) have their locations promoted with a star printed on a centerfold map in the town's weekly newspaper.

Items for sale include house and garden plants, baby clothes, high chairs, strollers, clothing, and tools. Local pottery and graphic artists set out their original goods. Food vendors bring their carts to feed the hungry and refresh the thirsty. Crowds are large and

Displaying Garments

Put all garments on hangers suspended from sturdy racks. It is possible to hang these items from a rope strung between trees or across the available space but rope tends to sag and allows the items to bunch in the middle. A rigid festive. Many out-of-the-area yard sale junkies consider Crestline a great place for annual outings.

Neither Memorial Day nor Labor Day offered me the right timing for my move that was scheduled to get me to The Palms by September 1. My sale would have had to take place in early August. And I had a further problem. Though I had a number of pieces to sell, I didn't have enough for a full-scale yard sale.

My salvation was a friend who promised to arrive at my home a day or two before moving day to remove my surplus for his participation in Crestline's annual Labor Day Sale. He picked up a microwave and a toaster oven, a coffee table, an occasional chair, and a wheeled shopping cart.

He was grateful for my offer of 50 percent of the take, and this relieved me of the responsibility of holding a sale at a time when I was busy moving. You, too, may be able to place your excess pieces on consignment with a friend or neighbor. Ask around. Most yard sale entrepreneurs are happy to handle items that add variety to their events.

metal rack or pole is much better. Linens, blankets, scarves, and towels are more easily seen if draped over the rack or clothes-pinned to hangers.

Wire hangers of the kind we get from dry cleaners have a way of breeding in my closets, but if you do not have enough, ask friends and neighbors for their throwaways.

I was able to use both wire and sturdy plastic hangers at one pre-move sale. As I took garments from my closet I packed the clothing I wanted to keep in suitcases and boxes. The sale items went into large plastic bags for transport to the sale site. This freed some hangers for use at the sale. I retrieved my favorite hangers afterward.

Even T-shirts should be separately hung for best display. No matter how neatly you fold and stack them on a vending table, the pile will become a multicolored mess as soon as the first customer sorts through them.

If you are selling a large number of garments of different sizes, check to see that the printed size tag remains readable. Add a stick-on size label if needed. This will save you time and the frustration of answering questions from customers across a crowded sale space. With luck, you will be busy taking money or dealing with a dedicated bargainer.

Appliances

Group appliances near an electrical outlet or string a long extension cord from a house outlet to your sale area so the appliances can be tested.

If a toaster doesn't work, don't claim that it does. Put a sign on it: "Needs Repair." It is surprising how many fixer-upper types are challenged by the expectation of being able to bring a simple appliance back to life.

Almost Anything Will Sell!

Do not underestimate the creativity of customers. A browser picked up my no-longer-needed, plastic footstool.

He turned it over and counted the eight pockets on the bottom formed by the molded cross supports. He gladly paid the $2 price saying it was perfect to store different size nuts and bolts and explained how he would drill holes in the legs and affix the unit upside down above his workbench.

In our latest three-family sale, friend Alma was selling a bedroom set that included a large mirror. She decided to move the mirror outside the garage for better display but she tripped. The mirror shattered. Alma was not hurt and the three of us hastened to gather the slabs of mirror into a large plastic wastebasket. Unbelievably, later in the day, not only did we sell the mirror frame, but we also sold the bucket of glass shards to an artist who does mosaics and collages.

Accessories and Supplies

A coat tree is excellent for displaying hats, purses and belts. These items may also be hung on hooks or nails probably already driven into the walls of the garage. Upturned boxes, porch steps or benches are good places for shoes. If you heap them in a box, you will have to keep picking them up from where customers drop them as they sort through the pile.

If you have many big or heavy items, borrow or rent a handtruck or dolly. These back-saving devices are available at equipment rental establishments. Collect plastic or paper sacks from grocery shopping. Having bags available in which customers may collect items encourages extra sales. These sacks are also the ones they will use to carry away their purchases—after they have paid for them.

Which brings us to pricing. Buy small, pressure-sensitive labels to put a price on *every* item. If you don't you will have a chorus of customers calling, "How much is this?" as they wave an item above their heads. Price your goods in even amounts: 50¢, $1, $5, etc.

Lawn chairs and camp stools come in handy. It is to your advantage to invite weary customers to sit. As the day wears on toward closing time, you and your vendor partners will also welcome a place to relax.

Staffing

You can probably do all pricing and display organizing by yourself, but get at least one other person to help while the sale is going on. To my knowledge, I have never lost anything to a shoplifter, but it is very difficult for one person to watch the premises, answer questions, and make sales at the same time, especially during the first hour that brings a flood of customers.

You and your helper will each need a vendor's apron, cargo pants, or any garment with several accessible front pockets to hold the bills and coins you will need to make change. Each staff helper should be supplied with change, about $25 to $50 each—a few $5 bills, but mostly one-dollar bills.

Color Coding

If your moving sale includes only your items, all the revenue goes into your apron. However, if two or more vendors are involved, each selling her own items, you will

Preventing Stuff Overload

Shoko Ohara, author of scores of cookbooks published in English and Japanese, reports that for every new piece of clothing she buys, she gets rid of another piece. As soon as she has finished reading a book, she gives it to a friend—both are great ways to keep your life uncluttered.

do well to color code the price tags. Ideally, Vendor Blue can accept pay for an item that belongs to Vendor Green, putting the money into the apron pocket reserved for that person's sold items.

However, depending on the size of the sales area, it may be simpler to direct the customer to pay Vendor Blue or Vendor Green, etc.—whoever was the original owner of the goods.

Boxed Items

While I advised that every item should bear a price, there are exceptions. It helps sales if you set out boxes of flexibly priced items. This does not mean you are changing price labels through the day.

Label boxes with signs: "50¢," "$1" and "FREE." Into these boxes go odd kitchen utensils, unmatched teacups, mugs, drinking glasses, attractive small containers, tiny pots, and bric-a-brac that you do not have space for in your new home or that you no longer want. As the day progresses, items in these boxes can be graduated from one box to another.

A customer may say, "I found this in the dollar box." Take his word for it, even if you remember putting it in the two-dollar box.

By late in the day, you may want to move all remaining items to the free box. Remember our motto: Get Rid of Stuff.

The Last Hurrah

The end of the stuff sale day comes. Some items did not sell. At our last sale, even the free box still held a ruler, a 3-hole binder I had neatly covered with contact paper, and one of those little gadgets that cores an apple. Place mats and several T-shirts and dresses were still on the rack. My almost-new electric blanket—an anathema on the Central Coast—still lay in its plastic bag.

Do not despair, somebody will come to clear out such items. Goodwill, the Salvation Army, and a number of other charity and church organizations are often happy to send a truck and driver to take whatever is left from your sale.

When you talk to the person in charge of picking up unsold items, be sure to describe any that are large or heavy. Due to possible injuries to their workmen, some organizations will not pick up excessively heavy or bulky furniture.

It's great if your sale places your unneeded items in the hands of those who will use and enjoy them, but the real rewards for you are the acquisition of both extra cash and a sense of freedom.

Use the following list to make sure your sale is both successful and fun.

Checklist for the Stuff Sale

- Select the date, preferably a weekend; consider the weather.
- Save plastic and paper bags for customer use.
- Advertise the location three to five days in advance.
- Get at least one person to assist.
- Stock a supply of bills and coins for making change.
- Borrow or rent a handtruck for heavy items.
- Allow time to prepare displays and group like items.
- Put appliances near an outlet.
- Mark prices on everything except for sundry items that go into boxes marked with one price applicable to each item.
- Call a charity organization to collect leftovers.

10

Shape Up and Move Out

You've pared down your belongings as a result of loot parties and the stuff sale, yet, at this point, you may still feel somewhat baffled as you survey stacks of cardboard cartons and plastic-sack blobs. Where did all this stuff come from?

Your home has taken on the appearance of a warehouse. The sacks (labeled, of course), you will recall, contain the clothing, towels, bed linens, blankets and pillows you will not need during these last few days before the big event. The boxes teeter in stacks from corner to corner reminiscent of a famous Italian landmark.

About the only familiar pieces still in place are your TV and your favorite chair. With all this confusion, your bird, your cat, or your dog—if these are a part of your life—will be especially needful of your attention and reassurance, and giving it to them will provide the same for you.

Items for sale on consignment by your friend—such as the microwave, toaster oven, and blender—will be picked up a day or two before the move. Which brings us to this question. If you pack, give away, or sell all your dishes and furnishings before you move, how do you manage meals and normal functioning during these last days?

Camping Out In Your Own Home

If you have ever gone camping, especially backpack-ing where you must carry all food, clothing, utensils and sleeping gear on your back, you will recall the need to travel light. If you have never indulged in any kind of camping, it may surprise you to learn how few toiletries, clothing, bed-ding, and cooking pots are essential for your daily needs.

Normally, you will not have given away or sold your refrigerator, range, or washer and dryer. In most instances, if you are leasing your home, some or all of these appli-ances remain with it. If your destination requires that you take them along, they will be disconnected and loaded by movers or gracious helpers on the last day. The moving in-structions furnished by a moving company will include in-formation about disconnecting appliances. Make sure a knowledgeable person does this. Failing to properly drain washing machine hoses and ice maker plumbing can result in extra messes to clean up.

Home Camping—Kitchen

Let's say you are single and have five days until move-out. On the first day of that countdown, pack everything but the following: a coffeemaker (if required), one small pot to boil water for tea or to cook cereal or vegetables, a small fry pan, a plastic bowl and a set of eating utensils, a sharp knife and a tablespoon. Retain paper plates (from the loot party), a coffee mug, and plastic drinking cups. Paper towels, handy for many last-minute chores, can be used as napkins.

Home Camping—Clothing

Make your own choices and adjust this list for the length of time you will be in transit and for any changes in climate between *here* and *there*. For the five days before move-out, basic essentials are: underwear, nightwear, comfortable shoes, a pair of work pants and top, a second pants and top or other garment for travel or for errands away from the house, a jacket (depending on weather), your medications, toiletries, and a couple of towels.

Pack these in the same bag you would take on a short vacation trip. All other clothing and incidentals can be boxed, placed in suitcases, plastic sacks, or left in garment bags in the closet until final day. You can always use the public laundry if necessary during your last week before the move.

Tidy-Up Concerns

Clear the fridge and clean it at least two days before your move. You may want to freeze a container or two of water to use in a food cooler for the perishables—perhaps milk or pet food—for your last day in the home. Neighbors are usually happy to have gleanings from your fridge, but you will be too busy the last few hours to deliver the quarter pound of butter, the stalk of celery, and the half-quart of milk. Such chores involve conversation which you do not have time for. Take your leftovers to neighbors and say your good-byes at least two days before Move Day.

Confessing my greatest fridge faux pas may be useful here. On one move, to save the renter electricity before he took over the home a week after I left it, I cleaned the refrigerator and turned off the power but failed to leave the fridge door open. The tenant sent me a bill for mildew removal. My intentions were good, but the execution was brainless.

Clean the bathroom using the cleansers you have held back from the large container of soaps and implements already packed. Put these in a box or plastic sack labeled for the room they are to go to at the new location. Keep the vacuum handy so that you, a neighbor, or a hired helper can do the last minute touch-up. The friend whose husband took some of my furnishings on consignment brought her own machine and vacuumed for me the day after I left. I had given her a key and she delivered it to the real estate firm that handled the rental of my home.

Vital Items

For all my moves, certain items always ride with me in my own car. You will have your own list of valuables (and pets) that you want to keep in your possession, whether you are flying, traveling by train, bus, or auto.

The items to be moved in my car are precious glassware, cameras, computer, television set, VCR, the file of vital paper documents, and information pertinent to the move and the arrival. (As noted earlier, safe deposit items have already been placed in the new box.) Also in my car kit are medications, toiletries, and a change of clothing. These are the same items I'd pack if I were taking a flight across the country and did not know for sure that my baggage would arrive when I did. Vital provisions remain within reach during transit from old to new.

Not all those who move to another location during the better-half-of-life have computers. Until 1985, I considered such magic-window boxes a fad that would pass and thought my electric typewriter would serve me indefinitely.

Once I had used a computer, however, I realized its value in speeding composition and storage of documents and manuscripts. Protecting it and any precious information it stores is essential. For insurance (since I can't guarantee that my car and person will arrive completely intact) I send disk copies of important computer records ahead by insured mail or other safe carrier.

If professional movers are handling computers, they will use special padding to protect this gear. Make sure these pieces are itemized and included in the insurance package offered.

Long-Haul vs. Short-Haul Move

My longest move was from Georgia to California. This was at the end of WW II. We packaged and shipped by rail the few possessions we owned at the time and drove the distance in our '37 Chevrolet. With the move from the Los Angeles Basin to the San Joaquin Valley, we used a small utility trailer. Additional community to community moves within California were made with the use of a U-Haul or other rental truck.

Subsequent moves were shorter. I engaged a professional mover for only one of these. For the others a nonprofessional crew did the job under my supervision. Each required different packing strategies and different transport vehicles. All have brought learning experiences—including the clamity of uninsured breakage. No two moves are alike.

Professional Van Line Move

Professional movers are a wonderful luxury, especially on long-haul moves. Yet, moves by professional van lines are costly—much more expensive than the do-it-yourself kind.

It is to your advantage, for the safety of your goods, to have the professional movers do the packaging. Their insurance will not cover anything you have packed yourself.

And, let's hope that your long-haul move, if aided by a professional van line, will not duplicate Ellen's, during which the diligent movers packed even her garbage.

The United States Department of Transportation recommends getting estimates from at least three moving companies. Inquire whether the price for the move over the distance you and your household are traveling is guaranteed or if the company has certain conditions that require extra fees—weather delays, breakdowns, etc.

Ask the company for a copy of "Mover's Rights and Responsibilities." Your mover should give you a list of helpful hints, advise you of insurance requirements, and provide boxes for packing. The company will also furnish any equipment it needs such as a dolly or handtruck for moving heavy pieces and quilted furniture wraps.

The Walk Through

Do not leave your premises until the moving company has loaded all your gear. Ask for a walk-through with the driver to make sure everything is on board. Check every closet and cupboard.

Arrange with the driver to coordinate your arrival and his at the destination. Give him a cell phone number to reach you en route or a telephone number at the destination in the event he has problems finding the right address or apartment number.

You—or an authorized representative—should be at the destination to receive your goods. If you drive your own car to the new location, you will probably arrive before the moving van, as trucks in most states are held to a slower speed than passenger cars.

On arrival of your goods, personally check (or ask the driver to check) the interior of the van to make sure all your possessions have been removed.

If you wish to have your car shipped by the movers and if it will not fit inside the van line vehicle with the rest of your belongings, it may be shipped on a large auto-transport trailer—the same as used to deliver autos to dealers.

Do-It-Yourself Moving

I have been licensed to drive since I was fourteen years old and have gripped steering wheels—albeit with white knuckles—in Paris, Rome, and London, as well as Atlanta and the labyrinth of freeways in Los Angeles and San Francisco. Though I'm eager to try many new adventures, I'm saving scaling the Matterhorn, sky diving—and truck driving—for my next incarnation.

My friend Emily is braver than I. With far less experience she set off for California from West Virginia carrying the family's entire household of furnishings in a twenty-four-foot U-Haul.

Fearful as she was, it was her first choice of the two available. She preferred that her husband be the one to remain behind to sell the house. Her teenage daughter accompanied her. "Mom was so frightened of merging traffic on freeways and off-ramps that I had to be absolutely silent during all lane changes." They made it without mishap and by the end of the trip Emily was merging like a pro.

I have always driven my own car and traveled in tandem with the relative or friend driving the van that carries my household goods. It is also possible to rent a tow-bar for the car or to mount it on a trailer that is towed behind the van. Costs are provided in brochures from U-Haul and other self-moving companies.

My major moves in the past eight years have been blessed with the skills of a capable truck-savvy son. He can use the money and I'd rather pay him than professional movers. With sufficient notice, he has been able to take a couple of days off from his job to help me.

We work well together. He knows from experience that by the time Move Day arrives, I will have gathered all possessions into boxes, plastic sacks, or suitcases and that his main job will be to plan the arrangement of large pieces for balance, load the works, and drive the monster truck.

Over the course of the various moves he has helped with, I have pared belongings down from the load that required a twenty-four-foot U-Haul to the one needing a seventeen-footer and to the last one which required only a pickup truck.

Making the Drive to Your New Location Safe and Uneventful

• Have your car thoroughly checked by a trusted mechanic: tires, fluid levels, battery, and fan belts.

• Check to see if your insurance covers tow service. What is the limit on how far you can have your car towed and still be reimbursed?

• Fill up before you leave, and watch the fuel level, stopping only in the daytime or at well-lighted, busy stations.

• Provide the destination phone number to a reliable person before leaving, and promise to call when you arrive.

• Telephone your estimated time of arrival to those at your destination so they will be watching for you.

• Use your cell phone for emergency service only. Use of a cell phone while driving in unfamiliar territory is too distractive.

• Do not drive unfamiliar roads at night.

• Do not stop to use an ATM. (Gray-haired women—or men!—alone are easy targets.)

• Keep the visible interior of your car clear of travel luggage. Keep maps folded except when in use. In other words, don't openly display the fact that you are in transit. Appearing to be out of your home area somehow suggests a vulnerability that may attract unwanted attention.

Engaging The Self-Moving Van

Truck and trailer rental companies' equipment may be driven or towed from one city to another by any licensed driver and does not have to be returned to the place of origin.

Charges are usually figured by the day and by the miles driven. A refundable deposit is usually required. Most companies offer insurance packages and instructions.

Handtrucks to help you with loading and protective pads to place over your furniture will also be available for rental. For my self-moves, we have rented only one bundle of six pads, because my plastic sacks of soft goods served as excellent spacers between furniture pieces.

Don't forget to get the address (and directions), the phone number, and the hours of operation at the location where the empty truck or trailer is to be dropped off when you won't be returning it to the location you rented it from. A late arrival may mean the delivery location is closed and you will be charged for an extra day.

The gas tank should be full at the time the driver picks up the vehicle, and it is the driver's obligation to refill it before delivering it to the company's lot at the destination. If refilling the tank is left to the destination's rental establishment, a premium charge per gallon is assessed.

Your rental company employee should make certain that the gas gauge, speedometer, radio and heater in the rental truck are working before you complete the agreement. On one trip, my son led off in the big rental van and cruised along at about 70 m.p.h.—too fast for the posted limit. This was unusual for him. At our coffee break stop, I learned that the truck's speedometer was broken. Our solution was for me to drive ahead at the truck speed limit. We arrived safely without mishap or ticket.

Relatively Speaking

At my son's direction, I had purchased a skein of rope and a roll of duct tape. We needed the rope to secure the frame of the sofa bed to prevent its unfolding as we loaded and unloaded it. The tape sealed the drawers of my metal desk and metal filing cabinet. He covered my walnut chests with blankets that he bound to the chests with the removable duct tape. After five moves, these chests remain in perfect condition.

On arrival at The Palms, by prior arrangement, we unloaded beds and overnight cases into my immaculate third-floor apartment. I was surprised to find that my brother had driven from Sacramento to help in unloading. After the two men maneuvered my entertainment center and heavy desk up the last six steps from the elevator into my apartment, my brother warned, "The next time you move, you'll have to get a new set of relatives."

He was joking, of course, but by the next move, I had disposed of the heavy pieces and did not need to call on any friends or relatives.

The Palms offered the location that was best for me in climate and proximity to family, cultural events, and recreational attractions. The next three moves kept me in the same general location but were made as adjustments for convenience and financial concerns.

Recreating a home within new walls and adjusting to

new neighbors and a new community are always challenging. But again and again, meeting these challenges taught me that my moves weren't the madness some suspected but a way of trying and trying until I get it right.

Last Few Days Before Your Move Checklist

- If you have large items to move, decide if you will use a commercial mover or rent a truck or trailer.
- Get estimates from three commercial moving companies and review their contracts before engaging one.
- Make certain you understand the moving company or rental firm's contract before signing it.
- Pack everything except what you need for survival during the last few days.
- Package delicate items for shipment in your own car or make sure they are on the commercial van line's insured list.
- Save a few cleanup supplies and tools to be packaged last.
- Double check the premises you are leaving and plan for an authorized receiver of your goods at your destination when using a commercial mover.

11

Turning New Corners and Making New Friends

Usually there's some apprehension and not a few surprises as we turn corners in our lives. We're not sure whether we'll welcome the new or be intimidated by it.

The threat of boredom and loneliness is a common concern. Whether your new location is mountain or seashore, city or country, you will be bored or lonely *only if you choose to be*. More new friends, organizations, churches, recreational options, libraries, galleries, and other cultural attractions are usually available than you will have time to explore.

Getting Acquainted with Your Retirement Home

When your latest turn brings you into a retirement complex, you are in for many benefits. Most of us, at our former homes, carried out the garbage, watered the garden, shopped for meals, cooked and washed the dishes—among countless other chores both pleasant and not-so-pleasant.

But, at homes dedicated to the comfort and pleasure of seniors, most household chores are taken care of by the staff.

These services are part of the package you pay for in a monthly fee. Adjusting to so many perks and such pampering may take a little time.

In selecting a living accommodation especially designed for seniors, applicants know in advance the cost and the amenities available, because they have toured the facility and evaluated it, paid the fees, and received lots of literature. Some retirement homes are like apartment complexes—two or three stories high. More elaborate and expensive are groupings of individual cottages.

Rooms are usually smaller than those we are accustomed to back home, but they are planned for efficiency and carefree living. As noted earlier, I chose The Palms, one of three adjacent residential complexes that comprise The Villages in San Luis Obispo, California, near the Central Coast. Though more expensive than many such senior residential homes farther inland, this area was my choice for its pleasant year-round climate, its accessibility to my children, and the community's many cultural and recreational attractions.

One- and two-bedroom units in this independent living facility range in size from about 400 square feet up to 900 square feet; some come with kitchens.

For about $200 less per month, I could have gone to a newly opened retirement complex in one of my former hometowns, Porterville.

There, at Sierra Hills, one of 260 Holiday Retirement Corporation-managed facilities, the perks include three meals a day and weekly maid service—linens furnished and laundered. Even light bulbs and toilet paper are provided, and all utilities, except telephone, are paid.

By prior arrangement, family visitors can be accommodated on premises. The firm's travel service includes arrangements for staying at (on a space-available basis) any of the Holiday Corporation's installations managed by Holiday Retirement Corporation in the United States (including Hawaii), Canada, and England.

Counting The Blessings

At The Palms, as with the Holiday Retirement Corporation's units, no lease is required. I did not face a penalty if I changed my mind, though occupancy of any duration would have required a cleaning fee on departure.

My contract involved paying, in advance, a security deposit equal to one month's rent. Two meals a day, seven days a week were included, as was free transportation to any destination within the city limits. All utilities except telephone and cable TV were included in the monthly fee.

Should I not have felt well enough on any given day to go to the dining room, I could have meals delivered to my door. Residents who enjoy cooking as a creative outlet, and those on special diets, may select an apartment that has a kitchen. However, at The Villages, vegetarian menus are available and included as part of the total package.

A Georgia retiree writes: "At my retirement home my life is as busy or restful as I like. The choice is mine. My children are happy to know I'm here and safe and I do not add worry to their very full lives."

One fellow resident at The Palms earned a nickname, "Chipper Charlie." After retirement from the building trades, and before he moved to the senior complex, he cared for his wife through her terminal illness. During that time he perfected his baking skills and he missed his kitchen when he joined our group of retirees. However, for economy's sake, he chose an apartment without a kitchen.

To satisfy his culinary enthusiasms, he perfected a recipe for chocolate chip cookies and his favorite cornbread that he could bake to his satisfaction in a toaster oven set up in his apartment.

Settling In

You sank into your favorite chair weeks ago when you were overwhelmed with where you should begin packing for your move. Now, the morning after arrival at your new home, as you contemplate unpacking, you may drop into the same chair feeling thankful you brought this comfortable old friend. It may even be the only seating space available among your jumble of boxes.

You may feel alone and lonely, but, in most instances, you probably won't have time to concern yourself about it: A knock comes on the door. It's one of your new neighbors inviting you to join him or her for breakfast in the dining room.

Residents at a retirement home are free to be "loners" if they choose but are encouraged to be part of the residents' association and to take advantage of the many opportunities that are available for participation and enjoyment in the larger community.

Tenants may join with others in common endeavors, such as cribbage games, adult classes, political discussions, and day trips, or they may choose to just sit around and talk about what interests them—anything from ancestry in a foreign land, to sports, family, hobbies, investing—nearly every subject known to man.

Discovering the Extras

The rules and services of a retirement home—whether in California or Georgia—are documented in its literature. As I began to unpack boxes cushioned with newspaper, I dreaded the long trips down from the third story to the refuse bins located behind the building. I thumbed through the listing of services and instructions for my new home. To my relief, I learned that trash collection was a twice a week service—at my door. I needed only to package recyclables separately from food scraps. All those cardboard boxes were to be flattened, an easy job with my small kitchen knife, and they, too, would be picked up. Over breakfast with my new neighbor, I learned that bubble wrap and plastic "peanuts" would be happily accepted by a nearby photocopy and packaging service.

A call to the front desk (staffed twenty-four hours) would bring cordial help to lift or move furniture, hang paintings, or change a light bulb. Available were twenty-four-hour emergency service, laundry rooms, beauty salon, swimming pool, spa, exercise room, and an office for the visiting doctor. A bookmobile from the local library arrived weekly. Ah, the luxury! Home was never like this!

Along with other instructions was the one that told me to locate the emergency call button in my bathroom, and I was oriented to the workings of the waterproof pendant signaling device. These devices will instantly alert the front desk in event of illness or accident. The first test of the efficiency of this system came for me when the grandkids' curiosity about that funny button in the bathroom brought a Palms staff member to the door ready to haul me off to the hospital or deliver whatever emergency service I needed.

Blood pressure and flu shot clinics, as well as instructive talks on health care, are a regular offering at The Villages. Most retirement homes stress health-awareness and provide transportation for medical and dental appointments, for shopping, banking, and to church and recreations such as concerts, museum visits, and socializing with the Out-To-Lunch Bunch.

In Your Spare Time

With no grocery shopping or housekeeping to do, you will have more time to read, knit, phone the kids, and explore. That never-realized vow to walk daily is now doable. If you haven't yet organized your photographs or begun recording family history, now is the time. What are your other interests: art, bingo, bridge, crochet, knitting, dancing, drama, education, hiking, genealogy, opera? The list of opportunities for participation is nearly endless.

A ninety-year-old at The Palms is a champion bridge player. She and others hold weekly games, and once a month they invite faculty wives from the nearby college to make up four tables that integrate the seniors and the younger members. If your special talent is making dollhouses or weaving horsehair coasters and you find no compatible soul next door, let your hobby be known. News travels fast when you're among seniors with lots of time to enjoy the better halves of their lives.

Transportation

As indicated above, most retirement complexes offer free transportation within the local area. For those who keep their cars, The Villages provide a large, lighted parking lot for residents' and guests' automobiles and a limited number of covered garage spaces.

If you have brought your car to your new location, you will probably want to orient yourself to your community by driving the streets. Fill the tank with gas and have fun getting lost. Your map from the chamber of commerce (or the front desk of your complex) will help you find key locations.

More Corners To Turn

If your move has brought you to a private apartment or house rather than a retirement center, you will have the same requirements for shopping, cooking, cleaning, and the clerical chores of paying utility bills that you had at your former home. It may take a little more time to work out managing these chores in your new area and in new circumstances. But lots of help is available.

Senior Centers

For all senior newcomers in a community, but especially for those without the retirement home support, an ideal early visit is to the local senior center. When I stepped through the doorway of the San Luis Obispo Senior Center for the first time, I was greeted by a cheery gentleman wearing a T-shirt inscribed: "Retiree: I Know It All and Have Plenty of Time To Talk About It."

One of his first instructions was that I register my change of address so that I could vote in the next election. He handed me a voter registration form (also available at post

The Pros & Cons
of Keeping Your Car

Transportation provided at most retirement complexes is extensive. Many residents find they no longer need their cars. This is also true for other super-adults who live in urban areas and can count on public transportation or hitching a ride with friends.

Selling your vehicle will bring in some cash, and the costs of insurance, licensing, fuel and maintenance are thus eliminated.

Bus, taxi, train transport or car rental for trips beyond the scope of the retirement complex's services may cost less per year than automobile ownership.

But frequent airplane flights, which are costly and usually require additional fees for ground transport at the destination, may make car ownership a less expensive alternative.

As I weighed whether or not to keep my car, I asked my trusted auto maintenance man for his opinion. He had recently tallied the records of servicing costs for twenty regular customers over a three-year period. Cars that had 100,000 to 200,000 miles on them averaged about $125 per month in upkeep, exclusive of fuel. With the added cost of insurance and licensing, ownership may not be the best plan. It certainly is something to think about.

Friends in my former mountain home are 300

miles away along good highways. I can drive the distance in less than six hours. Bus, rail, or a combination of the two would require twelve hours. And, the cost of the fares would exceed the cost of gas and oil for my car. Airline travel, even more expensive, would require renting a car at the destination airport or having a friend drive an hour to meet me.

As you tally the costs and your concerns about keeping your car, consider its age—and your own. Does driving unfamiliar streets make you nervous? Do you feel safe driving several hundred miles to visit distant children or your former home?

I am reminded of a news story about a woman who kept an inflated, life-size masculine figure beside her in the passenger seat as she traveled. She claimed "he" didn't talk back and created the illusion of protection.

Consider all eventualities. No matter how competent we feel, heightened awareness of traffic is an advantage at any age and particularly in our super-adult years.

As long as I feel comfortable driving, I want to keep my car for long-distance visits to relatives and friends. I enjoy driving alone with radio, music, or book tapes to keep me company. My car is in good condition and I always have it serviced on time. By the end of its reliable lifetime, I will be ready to leave the driving to others. On the other hand, I may look around for a used Porsche.

offices) and reminded me to go to the Department of Motor Vehicles to change the address on my driver's license. He also offered a small map with locations highlighted.

Most senior centers publish a monthly newsletter that lists various get-togethers such as potlucks, newcomer breakfasts, and card player groups. A nominal fee for membership will put you on their mailing list.

Widows and widowers in my area have their own association. If they remarry, they are kicked out of the club (kindly, of course) but are welcomed back for anniversary parties.

What else do you need in information or services: a reliable mechanic, gardener, handyman, optometrist, dentist, bridge partner, dog walker? If the senior center does not have the information, someone there can tell you where to find it.

Community Services

Still more information and opportunities are to be found at the office of Retired Seniors Volunteer Programs (RSVP), a nationwide organization whose gracious personnel take pleasure in providing information. Do not fear being immediately roped into volunteer work, though after visiting an RSVP office you may find a volunteer activity that suits you exactly.

Other nationwide organizations include Welcome Wagon, and various newcomer clubs—all listed in the phone directory. City Hostess, usually serving as an arm of the chamber of commerce, is publicized in most community newspapers with a telephone number. A representative will deliver maps, discount coupons, and, often, small gifts provided by local merchants. Newcomer groups and environmental groups such as the Sierra Club support special interest groups and offer many participatory programs—anything from quilting to bird watching. All are dedicated to welcoming you and making you feel at home.

The American Association of Retired Persons offers more services nationally for those fifty-five and older than there is space to list in this book. AARP chapters are active in virtually every community in the nation and telephone numbers are shown in all directories. The AARP is involved in many consumer and diversity issues, including those involving fraud prevention, wellness, managed care, public benefits, women, minorities, and people with disabilities. Membership, available to all citizens fifty and over at about ten dollars per year, covers a monthly bulletin and a bimonthly magazine and provides contacts for health, pharmacy, insurance, travel, and legal options, to name only a few services.

Further Education

In communities too small for a community college, high schools often sponsor evening adult education courses. Check these opportunities through the library or the chamber of commerce.

Four-year and community colleges normally provide facilities and may offer free noncredit classes for seniors in a wide variety of subjects, including art (oils, watercolor, photography), computer technology, even harmonica playing.

My local community college offers a class on how to compile your life story. An experienced instructor guides the group and many seniors form new friendships as they share information and strategies with fellow autobiographers.

Adult evening schools and colleges also offer opportunities for former teachers and others with special skills to share their learning. In a talk about the millennium, the Dalai Lama said, "Share your knowledge. It's the way to achieve immortality."

Financial management advice is available for those who have always left money matters to a no-longer-present partner. Ask for information on these services at a senior center.

Health experts typically recommend that the elderly stay active. Recent studies also suggest that simply mixing with other people may offer as great a benefit as regular exercise.

The Inevitability of Change

Moving our place of residence is not the easiest thing we will ever do. Even if we move fairly often, such disruption does not figure in our top ten favorite activities. But if the move is necessary, an attitude of acceptance for this new stage in our lives will make rounding the new corners conducive to both new pleasures and to personal growth and enlightenment.

My latest choice may not be my last. One never knows. But I do know that if I do move again, I will look upon the move as an adventure.

New Location Checklist

- Read any instructions furnished at your new facility completely.
- Check the location of onsite or community facilities such as the laundry or dry cleaners, beauty salon, and markets.
- Explore the neighborhood on foot.
- Read the residents' newsletter if one exists.
- Visit the local senior center.
- Check out public transportation and its costs. Even if you keep your car, you might prefer to use public transportation occasionally.
- Register your new address with the DMV and request a voter registration form at the post office or through the senior center.
- Visit the library and get a patron card.
- Check on classes and/or offer your skills at local education facilities.
- See the "Resources" section at the end of this book for ways to contact agencies that provide extensive information and assistance. Making use of these organizations' services is important for any retiree, but it is especially important for those who choose to live independently. The associations include, but are not limited to, the American Association of Retired Persons, the Area Agency on Aging, local chamber of commerces, City Hostess, community colleges, Elderhostel, Retired Senior Volunteer Program, and the Welcome Wagon.

12

Getting Settled

Settling into a Reduced Space

Experienced as I was with the requirements of moving my household, I still had much to learn—and gain—from my latest move. Since the move was from my own apartment to a bedroom in my friend Allison's home, I had to eliminate all but the most efficient pieces of furniture. The furnishings in my apartment living room, bedroom, bath and kitchen, a total of approximately 450 square feet, had to be reduced to fit a room and bath that totaled about 250 square feet. I didn't need a measuring tape to tell me that much had to go.

Vital to my daily needs were my desk, file cabinets, chest of drawers and a bed. My small entertainment center, bookcases, and a mahogany cabinet were also essentials as far as I was concerned, but the sofa, end tables, matched occasional chairs, and large lamps—all desirable in furnishing an apartment—needed to be sold or to go new homes.

Happily, I would no longer need pots, pans and dishes as I would have the use of Allison's large kitchen. As it turned out, the next tenant to occupy my apartment purchased most of my kitchen supplies. Allison's laundry facilities would also be available to me. This was a distinct advantage as I'd had been using a Laundromat during my tenancy in the apartment, a chore that always took time that I resented spending on it.

Decisions, Decisions

I knew where the end tables and the occasional chairs would go. They were destined for the daughter in Southern California, who had spoken for them at Mom's Loot Party long before. Transporting them to her was the next problem. When I priced the cost of shipping them by UPS or rail freight, shock set in. She could have purchased new pieces for less. The clerk at UPS suggested that I find a friend with a truck or van who could carry them. Great idea, but who?

We've all heard the admonition, "It's who you know...." Most such references pertain to career advancement but, for me, those whom I know are the vast number of people I've met in other than career-oriented venues.

When The Palms became too expensive for me and I began looking for different quarters, I learned of an apartment that was perfect for my needs at a meeting of fellow volunteers. Lesson: "Ask, and ye shall receive!" This belief was tested frequently in the ensuing months.

I searched my mind for other names in a wide range of contacts I'd made in the community. The young man who had rewired my apartment for my computer had told me he made frequent trips to Los Angeles. I called him and the deal was made. For less than half the UPS shipping cost, he carried the end tables and chairs on his next trip south in his van.

One son requested the cedar chest that had been a gift from my parents for my high school graduation. I was happy to keep it in the family and he came to get it. The thrift shop gained woolen sweaters I'd stored in the chest but rarely wore since moving to the warm climate.

Then there was the matter of my desk—metal with file drawers and a heavy super structure of shelves. It had followed me through the last eight moves and was in good condition but it would not fit into the new room if I were to have space for much else.

I advertised it for sale, planning to replace it with a smaller, more efficient unit. Not a single response came. Worse, neither the Salvation Army nor the local thrift shop would come for it. "Too heavy; liability risk...." Even if I had the skill and tools to dismantle it for the refuse truck, it hurt me to think of its winding up in the dump.

One week before move day, as I passed the local Barnes & Noble, I recalled that a number of the sales staff there were college students. Would someone there with the muscle to move it need my desk? I approached a young girl clerk, described the desk and asked if she knew anyone who might need it.

"I do," she beamed.

I gave her the desk in exchange for hauling it away. In addition, because she was looking for other furnishings for the house she was moving into, she purchased my coffee table, the chest of drawers, and a utility bookshelf.

The sofa and lamps were not a problem. One friend was furnishing a large home and could use them for her den.

Freeing Up Files

My two four-drawer file cabinets, each four and a half feet tall, were filled to the top, yet they were too bulky for the new quarters. They stored canceled checks, property records, insurance papers, family letters, and "precious" clippings. I'd stacked magazines and saved newspaper sections, always promising to sort, but never getting to the job. Now was the time.

We are advised to save canceled checks for five years. I had done so, but on a tip from my accountant I spent a half day going through these and destroyed all but the few that documented the items I had declared as deductible on my tax returns. This reduced five shoeboxes to an envelope.

My long writing career has produced hundreds of manuscripts, many unpublished, but worthy, I feel, of saving for possible future reference. One computer-guru son has advised me for years to "get rid of paper." The only manuscripts I needed to save in paper form were those from precomputer days. A day of weeding reduced these files by half. By concentrating on this organizing task until it was finished, I managed to consolidate important files into one cabinet. From the stacks of magazines and newspapers, I took the time to clip what I needed to save and threw out the bulky balance of these journals. I discarded the recipes I'd stored during this year I'd been again cooking for myself. Allison would be doing most of the cooking and had as many recipe books as either of us would ever need.

Saved greeting cards are another space hog. It always seems a waste to throw away these beautiful emblems of love. For years I have separated the art on Christmas cards from the personal messages. These I recycle as postcards at Christmas time. Cheap? Yes, they can be mailed at the postcard rate and I hope they brand me as a dedicated recycler—not a niggardly correspondent. Greeting cards for all seasons and birthdays are collected by charity organizations and used in art projects for children. Your library can direct you to these.

Sentimentality vs. Practicality

Sometimes there are things we just can't part with. A friend my age was seeking an apartment and when I told her I would be vacating mine, she came to see it. She loved it—until she saw the bedroom. While it housed my desk, single bed, file cabinets, dresser *and* my cedar chest, it was deemed much too small. Its total floor space was about the size of the canopied bed and headboard combination she loved and would not part with.

My own sentimentality came to the fore in several art pieces. I was fortunate that Allison admired two large framed watercolors painted by a mutual friend. I did not have to give them up. They now grace the walls of her spacious living room and I continue to enjoy them every day.

However, I had other art I wanted to keep—mainly the framed photos of children and grandchildren that had surrounded me on shelves, night stands, desk top and book cases for years. Several enlargements hung in apartment living room, bedroom and hall. The walls in my new room were mainly windows and the other space against them was needed for my desk, TV and dresser. The answer came when I passed a window display in a department store. A giant bulletin board held the photos of employees. Good idea! I removed my family members from their frames. They now greet me daily from the space-efficient bulletin board hanging above the chest of drawers in my office/bedroom/ living room. Allison welcomed my discarded frames. She uses them to hold the watercolors she paints and gives to friends and family.

Still, I had other precious things I did not want to part with. These included wood carvings made by one son; some ceramic pieces, a dozen albums of photos and a like number of metal cases housing photo transparencies that record my family's history.

This totaled about sixty cubic feet of goods of importance only to me. If I didn't decide how and where to store these valuables before moving day, I would have to stack them in the middle of my new room and hurdle the heap to get into bed.

In need of a small housewarming gift—a plant for Allison's garden—I visited a store that sold both nursery and building supplies. Wandering its spacious yard among the plants and trees for sale, I found an azalea bush for Allison and—more important—the answer to my storage needs. It was a weatherproof, heavy-duty plastic bin with a lid and wing doors in front. It would accommodate all the extras that I could not fit into my new room.

With Allison's permission, this large bin was delivered to her property. It sits beside the house in back in an unobtrusive location. As a precaution against mildew, I wrapped and sealed in plastic all items stored in this bin. A small additional purchase of a lock and hasp to secure the box and I was all set.

Help Is Everywhere

Overall, when you don't know how, where, when or what—*ask*! Most people—probably you included—delight in sharing knowledge gleaned from their life experiences. (Remember our man at the senior center whose T-shirt reads: "Retiree: I Know It All and Have Plenty of Time To Talk About It"?) Your sources of information do not have to be relatives or friends. They can be neighbors, local educational institutions, your pharmacist, or the clerk at the grocery store. Answers come from surprising sources.

Some of my most valuable contacts have been made through my hairdresser. The numbers of people who share their joys and woes with their beautician or barber make these people virtual encyclopedias of useful information. Almost every person you meet in today's changing world has moved at one time or another and has a warning or a triumph in his repertoire of moving experiences.

From addresses and phone numbers to yearly rainfalls, nearly any information you want is available on the Internet. If you do not own a computer to access this vast body of knowledge and information, ask your local research librarian for help. These Internet-savvy personnel are trained to pluck answers from worldwide sources. Most can print what they find for you to take with you.

Movers' Summary

Hundreds of options in geographic locations, types of housing, companions, and recreations are open to us all.

The national publication *Mature Living Choices* lists more than 1,200 communities in forty-six regional booklets (see the "Resources" section for ordering information) that span the country geographically. These housing options are geared to the special interests of retirees. More such communities are being built every day.

Obviously, hiring professional movers has much to be recommended. If you don't have the time or desire to pack or manage the move on your own, and the cost is acceptable, turn the whole project over to a moving company. This should make for a quicker and easier move. Your only stress may come with paying the bill.

If you decide to do most of the packing and the transport of your goods yourself, your efforts will likely take place over a period of time, ranging from a few days to a few weeks.

The lists at the end of the chapters in this book are designed to help you anticipate your needs and prioritize them. The priority for each chore should be established if you are to avoid last-minute rushing with its coinciding frustration.

It is both fortunate and challenging that not one of us knows what tomorrow will bring. Change is the only guaranteed constant in life. And, moving a household is one of the major changes. Look on it as an adventure and enjoy the experience.

With such a bounty of choices, you, too, may want to request that all correspondents "just pencil me in," so as not to ruin a whole page in their address books.

Happy moves to you!

Resources

The following is just a sampling of the many resources a sleuthing superadult can find on the Internet, at the library, or by asking at senior centers and elsewhere.

General Information Sources

Administration on Aging (AOA)
Office of External Affairs
330 Independence Ave. SW
Washington, D.C. 20201
Call (800)677-1116 to find local services.
Web site: www.aoa.dhhs.gov

AARP (American Association of Retired Persons)
601 E. Street, NW
Washington, D.C. 20049
(800) 424-3410
Web site: www.aarp.org

Area Agency on Aging (AAA)
There are many local Area Agency on Aging braches. Check the phone book or ask at a senior center.
601 E. Street, NW
Washington, D.C. 20049

Generations United
A national organization for promoting intergenerational policies, strategies, and programs.
122 C St. NW, Suite 820
Washington, D.C. 20001
(202) 638-1263
Website: www.gu.org

The National Council on Aging
409 Third Street, SW
Washington, D.C. 20024
(202) 479-1200
Web site: www.ncoa.org

The National Institute on Aging
NIA Information Center
P.O. Box 8057
Gaithersburg, MD 20898
(301) 496-1752
Web site: www.nih.gov/nia
Sources of Specific Information

American Volkssport Association
Sometimes called VolksWalkers or known by various local names.
1001 Pat Booker Road
Universal City, TX 78148
(800) 830-WALK
Web Site: www.ava.org

Ananda Village
An intentional community sponsoring classes and tours akin to its philosophy based on the teachings of Paramhansa Yogananda.
14618 Tyler Foote Road
Nevada City, CA 95959
(800) 346-4350
E-mail: ananda@ananda.org
Web site: www.ananda.org

Chambers of Commerce
Look for the address and phone number of the local chamber of commerce in the Yellow Pages.

Collaborative Rental Communities
Shared Living Resources Communities Information and Tours
2375 Shattuck Ave.
Berkeley, CA 94704
(510) 548-6608

Cut-Rate Cohousing (CRC)
1110 Bassi Dr.
San Luis Obispo, CA 93405
E-mail: bettykbranch@aol.com

Community Hostess
Contact your local chamber of commerce.

Creative Memories International
This firm also offers in-home business opportunities for those in-
terested in helping others collect and preserve family histories.
2815 Clearwater Rd.
St. Cloud, MN 56301
(800) 666-9344
Web site: www.creativememories.com

Cruise Jobs
Teachers, nurses, and recreational instructors are needed by most
cruise lines.
Contact this web site for job descriptions and information:
www.travelpage.com

Del Webb Retirement Communities
Nine multiunit communities in seven states, all oriented to seniors.
Individual ownership is offered, with temporary rentals available
for sampling locations and ambience. Contact the corporate office for information about the area that interests you.
6001 N. 24th St.
Phoenix, AZ 85016
(800) 385-0027
Web site: www.delwebb.com

Dockside Boat & Bed
These accommodations are for those wanting to sample a weekend or a few days aboard a docked yacht or small boat (breakfast
is delivered!).
419 Water St.
Oakland, CA 94607
(510) 444-5858
Web site: www.boatandbed.com

Elderhostel, Inc.
This organization offers worldwide tours and working vacations
for seniors.
11 Avenue de Lafayette
Boston, MA 0211-1746
(617) 426-7788
Web site: www.elderhostel.org

Fountain of Youth Spa & Recreational Vehicle Resort
10249 Coachella Canal Rd.
Niland, CA 92257
(888) 800-0772
Web site: www.foyspa.com

Holiday Retirement Corporation
Rentals specifically designed for senior retirees.
United States and British Columbia, Canada
P.O. Box 14111
Salem, OR 97309
(800) 322-0999

Holiswap
 Lists homes available worldwide for vacation home exchange.
Charged a small fee.
38 Allen St.
East Fremantle
Western Australia, Australia 6158
Web site: http://Holiswap.com

HUD (United States Department of Housing and Urban Development)
HUD has local services in every county in the United States.
451 7th St, SW
Washington, D.C. 20037

Humane Society of the United States
Priovides travel supplies, advice, and other information concerning companion animals. Check your local Yellow Pages.
Web site: www.hsus.org

Mail Boxes Etc.
Nationwide retail shops that do special packaging and mailing, provide mailing materials, and photocopy services. Check your local phone book.

Retired Senior Volunteer Program (RSVP)
Contact any senior center or see Uellow Pages for local information.
Room 9413
1201 New York Ave, NW

Washington, D.C. 20525
Seniors Home Exchange
For a fee, Seniors Home Exchange describes your home in an international directory and includes the home's proximity to cultural and recreational opportunities.
This is a web-based service.
Web site: www.seniorshomeexchange.com

The Villages
Consists of The Palms, The Oaks, Garden Creek and Sydney Creek. Serves both independent seniors and those requiring assistance.
The Villages of San Luis Obispo
55 Broad St.
San Luis Obispo, CA 93405
(805) 543-2300
(800) 676-8424
Web site: www.thevillagesofslo.com

VolksWalkers: See American Volkssport Association

Welcome Wagon
115 S. Service Road
Westbury, NY 11590
(800) 446-5627
Web site: www.welcomewagon.com

Magazines and Periodicals

Camperforce Directory
Lists more than 3000 campgrounds offering employment to RVers.
P.O. Box 1212
Cocoa, FL 32923
(407) 633-1091

Modern Maturity
Magazine published by American Association of Retired Persons. Source of information on travel, retirement homes and information for the over 50 group. Magazine comes gratis with membership in AARP.
AARP, Membership Center
P.O. Box 199
Long Beach, CA 90801-9925
(800) 303-4222

Mover's Rights & Responsibilities
Contact any major moving company in your area under "Movers" in the Yellow Pages for a copy of this brochure.

RV Buyers Guide
An annual list of all classes of RVs. Shows length, width, weight specifications and floor plans.
2575 Vista Del Mar Dr.
Ventura, CA 93001
(805) 667-4100
FAX (805) 667-4379

Where to Retire Magazine
Features many different retirement options and settings. Published five times per year.
Call to subscriber: (713) 974-6903
Web site: www.retirementmagazines.com

Workamper News
A bimonthly newsletter for full-time RVers who seek campground employment. Call for a free sample copy.
201 Hiram Rd.
Heber Springs, AK 72543
(800) 446-5627
E-mail: workamp@arkansas.net
Web site: www.workamp.com

Workers On Wheels
A bimonthly newsletter featuring articles about RVers and how they can make money on the road.
4012 S. Rainbow Blvd., Suite K94
Las Vegas, NV 89103
(800) 371-1440

Suggested Books

Most of the books listed below are available to be ordered through your favorite bookstore, but if you would rather order direct, contact information is listed.

Aging With Passionate Pleasure
by Gladys Hotchkiss,
A book that fulfills the promise of its title.
P.O. Box 1394
Crestline, CA 92325

Communities Directory: A Guide To Intentional Communities And Cooperative Living
Describes over 700 intentional communities in North America and around the world.
Fellowship For Intentional Community (FIC)
RR 1, Box 156
Rutledge, MO 63563
(660) 883-5545
(800) 462-8240
E-mail: fic@ic.org

Full-Time RVing
    by Bill & Jan Moeller
Trailer Life Books
2575 Vista Del Mar Drive
Ventura, CA 93001

Housemates' Handbook
    by Betty Branch,
1110 Bassi Dr.
San Luis Obispo, CA 93405
E-mail: bettykbranch@aol.com

It's Never Too Late to Be Happy!
Reparenting Yourself for Happiness (A Best Half of Life Book)
    by Muriel James
Quill Driver Books
1831 Industrial Way #101
Sanger, CA 93657
(800) 497-4909
E-mail: Orders@QuillDriverBooks.com
Web site: www.QuillDriverBooks.com

KOA Directory, Road Atlas and Kampground Guide
Gives information on campsites throughout the United States.
Meredith Integrated Marketing
1716 Locust
Des Moines, IA 50312
(515) 284-2258
(805) 667-4100

"Mature Living Choices"
Regional handbooks listing senior housing options—rentals, purchase, independent and assisted living throughout the U.S. and

British Columbia. For free copies featuring your preferred region, contact:
Mature Living Choices
Box 34062
San Antonio, TX 78265
Or FAX request to: (210) 655-2148.

Memory Manual: 10 Simple Things You Can Do to Improve Your Memory (A Best Half of Life Book)
   by Betty Fielding
Quill Driver Books
1831 Industrial Way #101
Sanger, CA 93657
(800) 497-4909
E-mail: Orders@QuillDriverBooks.com
Web site: www.QuillDriverBooks.com

Mover's Guide
A helpful booklet and kit of instructions and coupons available at all U.S. Post Offices.

That's Ex-Duffer Please!
A Guide to the Pleasures of Golf After 60 (A Best Half of Life Book)
   by Robert G. Faber
Quill Driver Books
1831 Industrial Way #101
Sanger, CA 93657
(800) 497-4909
E-mail: Orders@QuillDriverBooks.com
Web site: www.QuillDriverBooks.com

Index

Acknowledgments

It is a special pleasure to list here the names of those who have assisted me by contributing anecdotes, information and valuable critique during the research and writing of this book. I am especially indebted to San Luis Obispo NightWriters in general and specifically to Judy Abbott, Betty Branch, Myrt Cordon, Robert Davis, Ann Dozier, Nancy Ferraro, Laura Huffman, Fern Johnson, Karen Juran, Mel Lees, Jackie Mahoney, Vickie Meissner, Anne Peterson, Shirley Powell, Sharon Sutliff, and Barbara Wolcott. And to Shirley Hickman and Marilyn Meredith of Porterville Writer's Workshop; to Cora Breckenridge, Gladys Hotchkiss, Kathy Delong, and Ronnie Deasy of High Hopes Workshops, Crestline California; and to Carol Bachofner, Mike Foley, and Liz Pinto of Inland Empire Branch, California Writer's Club. Special assistance also came from Sandy Carpenter, Barbara Ciaramitaro, Sue and Will Dallons, Pat Dickson, Alan Gore, David Hinds, Maxine and Maurice Iverson, Wilma Miles, Lorry Newby, Diane Neilen, Jeri O'Neill, Patti and Mike Pruitt, Jim Simpson, Savitri and John Simpson, Laura and Tom Uhlmeyer, Ann Williams and Maret Willshon. My sincere thanks to all.

And appreciation to Steve Mettee, editor/publisher for faith, patience, and superior editing.

About the Author

Willma Willis Gore has moved home and hearth twenty times in her adult life—six times since she turned seventy. Her articles, essays, profiles and travel pieces have been published in more than seventy-five national and regional journals. Her photographs have illustrated most of her magazine articles, including several covers, and have been used in three of the nineteen children's books that bear her byline.

She has taught Write-To-Sell classes, done professional editing, and organized and led writer critique groups for more than twenty-five years. She is a conference speaker, a member of California Writers Club and San Luis Obispo NightWriters, and leads three critique workshops for that organization.